INSTITUTE OF PACIFIC RELATIONS
INQUIRY SERIES

THE INSTITUTE OF PACIFIC RELATIONS

The Institute of Pacific Relations is an unofficial and non-political body, founded in 1925 to facilitate the scientific study of the peoples of the Pacific Area. It is composed of National Councils in eleven countries.

The Institute as such and the National Councils of which it is composed are precluded from expressing an opinion on any aspect of national or international affairs; opinions expressed in this study are, therefore, purely individual.

NATIONAL COUNCILS OF THE INSTITUTE

American Council, Institute of Pacific Relations
Australian Institute of International Affairs
Canadian Institute of International Affairs
China Institute of Pacific Relations
Comité d'Etudes des Problèmes du Pacifique
Japanese Council, Institute of Pacific Relations
Netherlands-Netherlands Indies Council, Institute of Pacific Relations
New Zealand Institute of International Affairs
Philippine Council, Institute of Pacific Relations
Royal Institute of International Affairs
U.S.S.R. Council, Institute of Pacific Relations

POST-WAR WORLDS

POST-WAR WORLDS

By

P. E. CORBETT

*Professor of International Law
and Chairman of the Social
Sciences and Commerce
Group, McGill University*

I. P. R. INQUIRY SERIES

INTERNATIONAL SECRETARIAT
INSTITUTE OF PACIFIC RELATIONS
PUBLICATIONS OFFICE, 129 EAST 52ND STREET, NEW YORK
1942

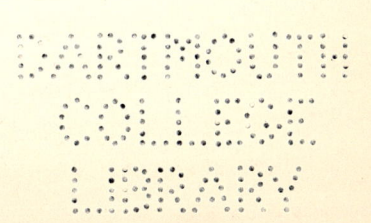

COPYRIGHT, 1942, BY THE SECRETARIAT, INSTITUTE OF PACIFIC RELATIONS
PRINTED IN THE UNITED STATES OF AMERICA
BY THE HADDON CRAFTSMEN, INC.

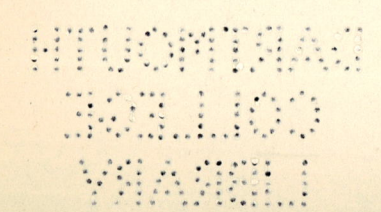

FOREWORD

This study forms part of the documentation of an Inquiry organized by the Institute of Pacific Relations into the problems arising from the conflict in the Far East.

It has been prepared by Dr. P. E. Corbett, Professor of International Law and Chairman of the Social Sciences and Commerce Group, McGill University; author of *Canada and World Politics* (with H. A. Smith, 1928), *The Settlement of Canadian-American Disputes* (1937).

The manuscript of this book was submitted to a large number of scholars in various parts of the world. Their criticisms were carefully considered by the author, and the text modified in many places. It is impossible to mention all who contributed to the study in this way, if only for the reason that some of them wish to remain anonymous. To select a few would be invidious. To any of them who may read this passage, the Institute and the author express their grateful thanks.

Though many of the comments received have been incorporated in the final text, the authorities referred to do not of course accept responsibility for the study. The statements of fact or of opinion appearing herein do not represent the views of the Institute of Pacific Relations or of the Pacific Council or of any of the National Councils. Such statements are made on the sole responsibility of the author. The Japanese Council has not found it possible to participate in the Inquiry, and assumes, therefore, no responsibility either for its results or for its organization.

During 1938 the Inquiry was carried on under the general direction of Dr. J. W. Dafoe as Chairman of the Pacific Council and in 1939 under his successor, Dr. Philip C. Jessup. Every member of the International Secretariat has contributed to the research and editorial work in connection with the Inquiry, but special mention should be made of Mr. W. L. Holland, Miss Kate Mitchell and Miss Hilda Austern, who have carried the major share of this responsibility.

In the general conduct of this Inquiry into the problems arising from the conflict in the Far East the Institute has benefited by the counsel of the following Advisers:

Professor H. F. Angus of the University of British Columbia
Dr. J. B. Condliffe of the University of California
M. Etienne Dennery of the Ecole des Sciences Politiques.

These Advisers have co-operated with the Chairman and the Secretary-General in an effort to insure that the publications issued in connection with the Inquiry conform to a proper standard of sound and impartial scholarship. Each manuscript has been submitted to at least two of the Advisers and although they do not necessarily subscribe to the statements or views in this or any of the studies, they consider this study to be a useful contribution to the subject of the Inquiry.

The purpose of this Inquiry is to relate unofficial scholarship to the problems arising from the present situation in the Far East. Its purpose is to provide members of the Institute in all countries and the members of I.P.R. Conferences with an impartial and constructive analysis of the situation in the Far East with a view to indicating the major issues which must be considered in any future adjustment of international relations in that area. To this end, the analysis will include an account of the economic and political conditions which produced the situation existing in July 1937, with respect to China, to Japan and to the other foreign Powers concerned; an evaluation of developments during the war period which appear to indicate important trends in the policies and programs of all the Powers in relation to the Far Eastern situation; and finally, an estimate of the principal political, economic and social conditions which may be expected in a post-war period, the possible forms of adjustment which might be applied under these conditions, and the effects of such adjustments upon the countries concerned.

The Inquiry does not propose to "document" a specific plan for dealing with the Far Eastern situation. Its aim is to focus available information on the present crisis in forms which will be useful to those who lack either the time or the expert knowledge to study the vast amount of material now appearing or already published in a number of languages. Attention may also be drawn to a series of studies on topics bearing on the Far Eastern situation which is being prepared by the Japanese Council. That series is being undertaken entirely independently of this Inquiry, and for its organization and publication the Japanese Council alone is responsible.

The present study, "Post-War Worlds," falls within the framework of the last of the four general groups of studies which it is proposed to make as follows:

I. The political and economic conditions which have contributed to the present course of the policies of Western Powers in the Far East; their territorial and economic interests; the effects on their Far Eastern policies of internal economic and political developments and of developments in their foreign policies vis-à-vis other parts of the world; the probable effects of the present conflict on their positions in the Far East; their changing attitudes and policies with respect to their future relations in that area.

II. The political and economic conditions which have contributed to the present course of Japanese foreign policy and possible important future developments; the extent to which Japan's policy toward China has been influenced by Japan's geographic conditions and material resources, by special features in the political and economic organization of Japan which directly or indirectly affect the formulation of her present foreign policy, by economic and political developments in China, by the external policies of other Powers affecting Japan; the principal political, economic and social factors which may be expected in a post-war Japan; possible and probable adjustments on the part of other nations which could aid in the solution of Japan's fundamental problems.

III. The political and economic conditions which have contributed to the present course of Chinese foreign policy and possible important future developments; Chinese unification and reconstruction, 1931-37, and steps leading toward the policy of united national resistance to Japan; the present degree of political cohesion and economic strength; effects of resistance and current developments on the position of foreign interests in China and changes in China's relations with foreign Powers; the principal political, economic and social factors which may be expected in a post-war China; possible and probable adjustments on the part of other nations which could aid in the solution of China's fundamental problems.

IV. Possible methods for the adjustment of specific problems, in the light of information and suggestions presented in the three studies outlined above; analysis of previous attempts at bilateral or multilateral adjustments of political and economic relations in the Pacific and causes of their success or failure; types of administrative procedures and controls already tried out and their relative effectiveness; the major issues likely to require international adjustment in a post-war period and the most hopeful methods which might be devised to meet them; necessary adjustments by the Powers concerned; the basic requirements of a practical system of international organization which could promote the security and peaceful development of the countries of the Pacific area.

EDWARD C. CARTER
Secretary-General

*New York,
November 15, 1941*

AUTHOR'S PREFACE

The purpose of this book is to examine the causes of the breakdown of the international institutions set up after the last war, to provide a summary of recent thought on ways and means of creating a more effective community of states in the future, to analyze the principal problems of authority and structure involved in supranational organization, and finally to sketch the essential agencies of an incipient world commonwealth.

Long before 1939, many observers had given warning of a second world war and busied themselves with plans to prevent it. Since September of that year, when Hitler's invasion of Poland was followed by declaration of war on the part of England and France, inquiries into the causes of the present conflict and proposals for its permanent settlement have multiplied. Most of these studies and the plans to which they lead have reference to one area only, Europe or the Atlantic or the Pacific. A few, perceiving early the intricate interdependence of the struggles going on in Europe and Asia, sketch in broad outline conditions of peace and a system of international organization for the world as a whole. Through them all runs the same fundamental idea—the boasted sovereignty of the state must be subordinated to the general interests of a human society which progress in science and technology has made universal. Their number and the wide variety of their source are evidence that the growth of an international mind has not been arrested by the collapse of the peace machinery of the 'twenties.

The history of the League of Nations shows that governments and peoples alike had failed to understand and so had not accepted the implications of even so conservative an inroad on the tradition of state sovereignty as the Covenant of 1919. Constantly in the course of carrying out the provisions of that instrument, proposals of action were met by the objection that the League was not intended to be a superstate and by insistence upon the surviving right of the states members to judge all issues for themselves. Thus were defeated the most significant attempts to settle international disputes by collective action, to achieve disarmament, to cope with economic and social inequalities, in a word to deal with the causes of war at their origin.

These are days which call stridently for action, and many of our contemporaries appear to regard this call as a dispensation from all thought which reaches out beyond the day's immediate task. Yet the injunction to leave to the day of victory and to the people's representatives then in power the study of the problems which will crowd upon us when hostilities have ceased is a shortsighted and a foolish one.

The reasons for intense preliminary study and wide general discussion are stated with the authority of direct personal experience by Mr. Harold Nicolson, recently Parliamentary Secretary to the Ministry of Information in Great Britain. Mr. Nicolson was a member of the British delegation at the Paris Peace Conference. In his book *Why Britain Is at War* he describes it as the fundamental error of that conference that no "very clear programme had been laid down in advance." The anger that had accumulated in four years of war, and the haste of the delegates to restore normal conditions, produced an atmosphere that stifled long-term calculation. The result was an unhappy compromise between two conflicting theses, one of which demanded a peace of force, the other a peace of justice. If we are to have long-term calculation (and surely it will be needed), then it had better begin now.

President Roosevelt, in his message to Congress on January 6, 1941, stated a noble objective, confirmed in the joint declaration which he issued with Mr. Churchill on August 14, 1941. But the two leaders had little to offer on the forms and institutions by which their declared aims are to be realized. That must be worked out by experts, and if their creation is to last it must be understood and accepted by the peoples. The more that can be done toward that end while the war is still in progress the better the chance will be of an enduring peace. We shall be fools indeed if we count upon the unrehearsed meetings of statesmen to produce a working constitution like the rabbit from a conjurer's hat.

The following chapters are an attempt to stimulate preparation for the arduous work of settlement that must follow the war. It may well be that, with the memory of 1919 in men's minds, no single conference will be entrusted with the structure of world order. A provisional regime, set up by the victors, may afford time for more patient and solid building. But care must be taken that the provisional mechanisms of control and administration are not of a kind to perpetuate animosities and prevent a definitive organization. An agreed design, known to the peoples concerned as the ultimate purpose, will elicit active collaboration. It will also influence the form and operation of interim agencies so that these may merge naturally into the "wider and permanent system of general security" contemplated by the Atlantic Charter.

CONTENTS

	Foreword	vii
	Author's Preface	xi
I.	World Anarchy	3
II.	The Labor of the 'Twenties	12
III.	Grand Designs	28
IV.	Ascendancy of the Federal Idea	42
V.	The Inter-American System	54
VI.	Peace in the Pacific	71
VII.	The Order of the Axis	83
VIII.	The British-American Front. Collaboration or Union?	89
IX.	Law and the Community of States	98
X.	Sovereignty and Nationalism versus the Community of States	108
XI.	Economic and Financial Organization	116
XII.	Supranational Police	136
XIII.	Supranational Courts	146
XIV.	Supranational Legislation and Peaceful Change	155
XV.	Supranational Administration	170
XVI.	Colonies and Mandates	177
XVII.	World Order	185
	Bibliography	197

POST-WAR WORLDS

CHAPTER I

WORLD ANARCHY

The Treaty of Versailles brought to an end the First World War and set up the League of Nations to secure perpetual peace. Now, a little more than twenty years after that inauguration of a "new era," wars rage once more in Europe, Africa, Asia. The great nations of the world are locked in one of those gigantic struggles which concentrate human strength, courage, invention and devotion on slaughter and destruction. In the conflict all the laws and institutions designed to govern the intercourse of states and to advance their recognized common interests are set aside. The clash of tooth and claw, magnified a million times by the refinements of civilized science and art, is once more the order of the day.

The root causes of this renewed battle reach far back through and beyond the war of 1914-1918. They are political, economic, social, and psychological in character—a complex of grievances, ambitions and fears woven into the history and the mentality of the belligerents.

Competition for possessions and privileges is a universal feature of human life. In those limited groups which we call states, it has been subjected to a control which roughly harmonizes the interest of the individual with that of the group. The political organization has been assisted in this task by morals and religion. But the morals which serve as a standard for individual conduct have never been held with any common conviction to apply to the state; and in their "sovereign" political groupings men have not yet been willing to submit to a universal law enforced by a common superstate authority.

Political organization does not completely eliminate war. Otherwise revolutions would be unknown. But it is the best method man has devised for preventing strife, and the better it is the rarer is revolution. If we accept the tendency to strife as inherent in the nature of man, then the frequency and scope of wars is due to our failure to adopt the method of political organization for the purpose of equipping a universal community and controling the conduct of nations as members thereof.

As the war proceeds the hope that saves many men, combatant and noncombatant alike, from despairing disgust is that when the fighting stops a serious effort at such organization will be made. The hope is encouraged by the fact that the Peace Conference of 1919 drew up a Covenant and established a League of Nations. The failure of that first attempt is not generally taken as proving that "collective security" is an illusion. On the contrary, there is a widespread movement among the peoples to insist that when the time comes the attempt must be repeated, and that we must profit by the inter-war experience to avoid errors now recognized in the structure and procedure of the League.

Meanwhile governments issue statements about the nature of the current war, its immediate causes, and the aims they have in mind as they fight it. These statements require some examination, as they are not quite without bearing on the prospect and the possible forms of post-war organization to preserve peace.

Nothing has served more commonly as a description of the war than the statement that it is a battle between democracy and totalitarianism. It actually began with an attack on Poland, which was hardly a consistent practitioner of democracy; and it has since brought in, on the democratic side, Greece and the Soviet Union, where dictatorship has surely been more familiar than representative government. Nevertheless, there is an element of truth in the description.

Certainly the British nations, and some at least of their allies, attach high value to the personal liberty of the citizen. Their theory of government is one which restricts that liberty only so far as is necessary to prevent it destroying like liberty in others. Nazism and Fascism, on the other hand, appear to insist that the happiness of the individual consists primarily in the greatness of his state. To magnify that greatness, they mobilize the citizen, assuming a minute control over his life.

There is ample evidence that, as they conquer a country, the Nazis impose their own methods of government. It is literally true that many of those fighting against them would rather die than submit to those methods. The war may therefore be accurately described as one between democracy and totalitarianism.

That, however, is only part of the story, and not the most essential part. From the beginning, the essential motive in resorting to arms against the Japanese, German and Italian aggressors has been to preserve the nationhood of the defenders. The simplest and truest definition of the war from the point of view of the countries aligned against the Axis Powers is that it is a war against conquest and conquerors. The attack upon Greece and the Soviet Union was no crusade of one doctrine of government against its opposite. The heroic defense in both cases has not been a championship of a political theory or even of a way of life. It has been a passionate effort to preserve soil and autonomy from an invader.

It is important that this truth should be clearly recognized. Some of the countries which will have contributed most to the defeat of Hitlerism might fight again to resist the imposition of democracy upon them. The purpose common to all the anti-Axis nations is that of choosing their own mode of life and government—a right which might with some reason claim title as the essence of international democracy, at least insofar as the choice is compatible with the peace and security of other nations.

The leaders of Germany, Italy and Japan, complaining that their peoples have been denied their just share in the lands and fruits of the world, have set out to take by force what they declare their due. After considerable preliminary successes, they announce their intention of imposing a more efficient political organization on Europe, Africa and Asia.

Asserting that neither welfare nor security can be attained with the present complex of sovereign states, that sovereignty and empire belong only to the strong, they propose that the world should be divided amongst two or three "master races" holding sway over the lesser breeds.

It may be conceded at once that peace and prosperity alike demand the breaking down of national barriers and rivalries. The grouping of states into one or more larger societies seems the only possible alternative to recurrent war and depression. That means submission to supranational authority. There are some, of course, who continue to believe in the state as the ideal and ultimate center of human authority; but for the most part the question which now divides opinion is not whether superstate organization is desirable but whether people in the mass have reached the degree of understanding necessary to accept and operate it.

The leadership of the great states is a condition precedent to the establishment of any supranational authority and to its successful working once it has been set up. The present war might well have been avoided if the United States had joined the League, or even if Great Britain and France, instead of following cross-purposes, had furnished a concerted direction. That, however, is quite a different thing from the Nazi contention that the required authority must take the form of dictation by "superior" races in the great regional divisions of the world.

In the beginning nation-states were ruled by powerful individuals or groups who imposed one will on the community. The course of political history since the middle ages has, however, been roughly a progress from this principle of authority to one of liberty. The United States of America, greatest of modern political communities, was able to take advantage of past experience and organize itself as a democracy. Must that larger community of nations which reason now demands pass through the evolutionary process from autocracy to popular government, or may it, by the intelligent use of accumulated knowledge, make the saving shortcut employed with such lasting results by the authors of the American Constitution?

British and American leaders have affirmed and reaffirmed their purpose to work for a free association of free peoples. They have expressed in unmistakable terms their abhorrence of the supranational dictatorships planned by Nazidom. Yet the detailed aims which they declare imply an effective association. Their objectives presuppose a form of supranational administration which, though it is to be set up and to operate by consent, will nevertheless be strong. They pose, on a universal plane, what has been the central problem of democracy in the state.

The aims stated by some standard-bearers of democracy go far beyond a mere organization to prevent war. In response to a growing demand among the British and American rank and file, they include rising standards of living and the spread of personal liberty throughout the world. A superficial interpretation of these declarations finds an apparent inconsistency. How can better living conditions and freedom of speech and religion be generalized without dictating the doctrine and practice of internal government? But dictation would be incompatible with supranational organization on democratic principles.

The inconsistency is only apparent. Given the variety of regimes now combined against the Axis and entitled to a voice in the peace when victory has been won, the United States and Great Britain will hardly be able to impose their particular philosophies and modes of government. But the creation of new institutions of world administration will give them an infinitely better chance of using their resources and their influence to further the social and spiritual objects of democracy.

Given the profound difference between the "new orders" of the Axis on the one side and the post-war worlds sketched by British and American statesmen on the other, the war becomes, in one of its many aspects, a struggle between two doctrines of supranational organization.

In his speech before the House of Commons on August

20, 1941, the Prime Minister of Great Britain declared that he would not now commit his government to any precise plan of post-war reconstruction. For Mr. Churchill the war in its present stage is one for the survival of Britain, and no division of opinion as to the structure of the world after victory must impair the unity of the national will in that immediate purpose. Nor, he might have added, would it be profitable to split Britain's allies into opposing camps on the problems of future readjustment.

Mr. Churchill's reserve has been interpreted in some quarters as a refusal to be bound even to the general principle of a new attempt to establish a democratic world order. Yet there is ample evidence, as the following analysis will show, that the British nations still persist in the aim, stated repeatedly in the early months of the war, to establish an effective society of nations.

On July 21, 1940, General Smuts, who has served on more than one great occasion as spokesman for the British Commonwealth, declared that the Commonwealth is fighting for a second opportunity to build a league, this time with a central force powerful enough to execute joint decisions. His broadcast from Capetown contained the following significant passage:

"The failure of the League of Nations was largely due to the absence of a central control which could harmonize the freedom of each with the proper functioning of the whole of human society. We therefore aim at a society of nations which will supply this defect and which will possess a central organization equipped with the necessary authority and powers to supervise the common interests of mankind. Intercourse between the nations will be free, and commerce, economics and finance will be freed from all hampering restrictions and obstructions. As between man and man there shall be social justice; as between nation and nation there shall be the rule of law, the absence of force and violence, and the maintenance of peace."

These are the words, not of an academic visionary, but of a responsible public man, one of the principal authors, as it happens, of that Covenant whose imperfections he now confesses. They set forth a program as ambitiously idealistic as any formulated by detached theorists. That program is being directly and indirectly confirmed from day to day by leaders of the peoples opposing the European and Asiatic aggressors.

In his message to Congress on January 6, 1941, President Roosevelt stated in general terms the peace aims of his Administration:

> In the future days, which we seek to make secure, we look forward to a world founded upon four essential human freedoms.
> The first is freedom of speech and expression—everywhere in the world.
> The second is freedom of every person to worship God in his own way—everywhere in the world.
> The third is freedom from want—which, translated into world terms, means economic understandings which will secure to every nation a healthy peacetime life for its inhabitants—everywhere in the world.
> The fourth is freedom from fear—which, translated into world terms, means a world-wide reduction of armaments to such a point and in such a thorough fashion that no nation will be in a position to commit an act of physical aggression against any neighbor—anywhere in the world.
> That is no vision of a distant millennium. It is a definite basis for a kind of world attainable in our own time and generation.

Again, in his broadcast of May 27, 1941, the President declared:

> We will accept only a world consecrated to freedom of speech and expression—freedom of every person to worship God in his own way—freedom from want—and freedom from terrorism.

Speaking for the British Government on May 29, 1941, Mr. Eden, the Foreign Secretary, said, "We have found in President Roosevelt's message to Congress in January, 1941, the keynote of our own purposes." After quoting with approval the President's statement regarding what have come to be known as "the four freedoms," the British Foreign Secretary went into some detail as to the method of securing freedom from want. "It will be our wish with others," he declared, "to prevent starvation after the armistice period, currency disorders throughout Europe, and wide fluctuations of employment, markets and prices, which caused so much misery for twenty years between the two wars." Referring then to a speech by Mr. Hull on May 18, 1941, he continued, "I echo Mr. Hull's admirable summing-up in a recent declaration when he said, 'Institutions and arrangements of international finance must be so set up that they lend aid to essential enterprises and continuous development of all countries and permit payment through the processes of trade consonant with the welfare of all countries.'"

The world cannot be secured from fear and want by words, however potent and however sincere the personages who utter them. What Mr. Sumner Welles said in his speech of July 22, 1941, on the matter of disarmament, might have been said with equal cogency about every other item on the President's four-point program—". . . the abolition of offensive armaments and the limitation and reduction of defensive armaments . . . can only be undertaken through some rigid form of international supervision and control. . . ." This means organization capable of executing joint decisions even against the will of a recalcitrant state.

The same implications are contained in the joint declaration issued by President Roosevelt and Mr. Churchill on August 14, 1941. This, the most authoritative statement of war aims to proceed thus far from the anti-Axis side, is modest in expression. It disowns any plan to make territorial changes without the free consent of the peoples concerned, thus repudiating the alleged plot to dismember Germany; it offers to all peoples the right to choose their own form of government; it wishes "to see sovereign rights and self-government restored to those who have been forcibly deprived of them." It promises an endeavor, subject only to existing obligations (such, presumably, as those set out in the surviving Ottawa Agreements), to secure equal access to trade and to raw materials for all states, victor and vanquished alike. It expresses the desire for international collaboration in the economic field, "with the object of securing for all improved labor standards, economic advancement and social security." It hopes, "after the final destruction of the Nazi tyranny," to see a peace established that will enable all men to live free of fear and want and to traverse the seas unhindered. Finally, it voices the conviction that "pending the establishment of a wider and permanent system of general security" nations which "threaten or may threaten aggression" must be disarmed.

Conspicuously absent is any explicit reference to freedom of expression and religion, possibly because some contradiction was apprehended between the spread of such liberties on the one hand and the promise of free choice of forms of government on the other. In other respects the declaration is substantially a repetition of the President's earlier utterances.

The machinery by which the expressed hopes and wishes are to be implemented is again left to inference. There is no mention in so many words of any association, league or union of states. The "wider and permanent system of general security" is so cautiously foreshadowed that it appears only as a possible future development pending which potential aggressors must be deprived of their weapons. The unprepared state of American opinion, plus Mr. Churchill's unwillingness at this stage of the war to be bound to a precise structural program, would be sufficient to account for this avoidance of "blueprints," quite apart from the fact that there are other governments to be consulted.

The August meeting of the President of the United States and the Prime Minister of Great Britain was not a constituent assembly for the drafting of a world constitution. Their declaration is nevertheless a joint commitment to use for the purposes stated the resources available when military victory has been won. It is a promise of action of a sort which presupposes powerful agencies of international administration and control.

Such are the foundations of the present hope for a strong new effort to bring order out of chaos. Similar hopes have existed before, and in 1919 institutions were created for their realization. Why did they fail?

CHAPTER II

THE LABOR OF THE 'TWENTIES

In 1919 the peoples of the world were thought to be weary enough of fighting or of the trials of neutrality to welcome a bold venture in international association to prevent war. They had little notion of the kind of institutions that would be needed, or of their relation to the traditional authority and functions of the state. All that they had was a vague conviction that life under the shadow of war was not good enough and that something had to be done about it. Groups of intellectuals in England, Holland, Scandinavia, and to some extent in France, Italy and even Germany, had been busy formulating plans for a league to enforce peace. In 1917 and 1918 individual officials or committees were appointed by some of the governments to prepare draft constitutions for a society of nations. But participation in these discussions was limited, and the official deliberations had been too late in beginning and too little co-ordinated to bring the principal governments into agreement on anything more than the desirability of some joint organization, to be directed by the Great Powers, for checking aggression. In the haste and conflict of the Peace Conference even this minimum of common purpose was saved only by the insistence of President Wilson. He insisted not only that a league must be established, but that its constitution must be inserted in the treaties of peace themselves.

The Covenant of the League of Nations was indeed set at the beginning of each treaty of peace. But it was not the covenant which Wilson himself or any other delegate had wished. Each delegation had presented proposals of its own, though even within the national groups at Paris there were wide differences of opinion both as to the merits of a league and as to its form and functions. The French proposed an international police, the Italians an international legislature and an economic commission to supervise the supply of food and raw materials. The United States and Great Britain joined in opposition to these ideas. Some delegates urged compulsory arbitration, others would have none of it. Wilson wanted the Germans admitted at once, the French refused. The Japanese, rankling over the exclusion of their nationals from immigration to the United States and British Dominions, pressed for a declaration of racial equality and were defeated by Anglo-American resistance. Even the most devoted advocates of a league, including Wilson himself, backed away in alarm from proposals, such as that of Japan, which would have authorized a supranational body to pry into the "domestic jurisdiction of states" or which, like those regarding international police and legislation, would have given to the organized world community the character of a superstate.

Apart from the difficult negotiations directly concerned with the future world order, the general temper of the conference was anything but propitious to measures for lasting peace. Both within and between delegations a bitter struggle waged between those who wanted retribution and who saw the means of immediate reconstruction and future security in economic, financial and territorial exactions from the defeated enemy, and those who desired speedy reconciliation and who believed that peace and recovery could only be achieved by willing and active co-operation between victors and vanquished. The delegates were politicians and their constituencies wanted an end of war, to be sure, but they also clamored for full payment of the immense bill of war damages, punishment of the guilty, and the permanent weakening of the German nation to a point where it could no longer nourish designs of conquest. Only a patient campaign of popular education could have persuaded the public, or indeed many of its representatives, that these demands were mutually destructive. But everywhere was haste—haste at home to demobilize and be rid of wartime restrictions and exactions, haste at Paris to return to familiar surroundings and the normal activities of political life. A few months must suffice, amid conflicting national ambitions and in an atmosphere of suspicion and hostility, to think out and give shape to an entirely new development in human relations which, if it was to endure at all, involved changes in the situation of authority and in the use of power greater than any that had ever before been consciously attempted.

In such turmoil was the League of Nations born. Little wonder if its constitution was marred by reservations of national sovereignty, by concessions to narrow political interest, and by showy undertakings that might mean much or nothing according to the subsequent will of the parties. The placing of the Covenant in the forefront of treaties whose injustice was to be the rallying cry for opponents of the new order was to prove a severe handicap on the League's mission of pacification. Yet if the experiment has been of any use—and I am one of those who believe that it accomplished things of lasting value, and who regard it even in its failures as an inestimable source of instruction for future efforts—we must thank this circumstance for it. If Wilson had not made the League a condition of the peace settlement as a whole, the delegates would have given up the attempt to draw any association of states at all from the battle over its scope, functions and authority.

The paper product of the conference was a batch of treaties, each beginning with the twenty-six articles of the Covenant of the League of Nations. In that document the members of the League—and eventually there were more than sixty of them—promised to protect each other's territory and independence. They agreed to reduce their armaments, to submit disputes to peaceful examination, and in no case to go to war until three months after decision or report. They undertook to cut off commercial and financial dealings with any state that broke its promises and went to war, and they authorized the Council of the League, composed of the Great Powers and a few smaller states elected from time to time, to recommend what military measures might be necessary to back up these economic sanctions.

The Assembly of the League, in which all the members were represented, was to advise the revision of treaties that had become unjust and the reform of conditions threatening peace. A Permanent Court of International Justice was set up at The Hague. The colonies taken from Germany and Turkey were handed over to League members to be administered in trust for the benefit of the inhabitants. Committees and offices were established with world-wide representation to prevent the spread of epidemics, to control the traffics in drugs and white slaves, and to improve conditions of labor. Each member was to give equitable treatment to the commerce of the others and there was to be freedom of communications between all of them. An expert secretariat was built up at Geneva with the appropriate offices and equipment.

It was the boldest international organization the world had ever seen. There were plenty of skeptics to ridicule the new utopia and predict its early dissolution; but for some years it was backed by popular support which politicians could not ignore. Government after government felt compelled to proclaim that the League was "the cornerstone of foreign policy." The American people's rejection of the Covenant brought bitter disappointment; but the setback was attributed to temporary factors in party politics, and the League set about its business hoping that its success would speedily bring the United States into the fold. And, in those early years, its work was not without results.

Sweden and Finland were in dispute over the Aaland Islands in the Gulf of Bothnia. A committee of the League decided that Finland had the stronger claim, and Sweden submitted with grace. Greece and Bulgaria were dashing headlong into a border war when the League intervened and arranged a settlement. Eastern Europe and the Balkans sputtered with boundary quarrels. The League patched them up. In Danzig the incessantly conflicting claims of Poland and the Free City were balanced short of violence;

and in the Saar Territory a difficult peace was maintained between French and Germans. At the same time watch was kept on the far-flung system of mandates in former German and Turkish territories, and on the treatment of racial minorities in Central and Eastern Europe.

Austria and Hungary, their territories chopped up and their industries and markets dislocated by the war and the treaties, were in desperate straits. The League raised loans for them, helped them to make the best of their diminished resources. It held economic conferences that pointed the way (though mostly to blind eyes) out of the depressions that gripped so many countries in the early 'twenties. It maintained a service of economic research and information that earned world-wide approbation.

The Health and Social divisions of the League carried on an increasingly successful battle against disease in Asia, Africa and South America, and the drug and white slave trades throughout the world. The International Labor Organization working in conjunction with the League and financed by it, got on with the huge job of shortening hours of work, protecting the health of the worker, limiting child labor, and generally improving the lot of the industrial employee. So important were the results obtained that the United States, though it rejected all invitations to enter the League or the Permanent Court, became a leading member of this organization.

From its first session in 1922 until 1940, the Permanent Court gave thirty-one judgments in disputes between nations. In addition it handed down twenty-seven advisory opinions in questions that might otherwise have degenerated into serious friction. These judgments and opinions, besides keeping the immediate peace, helped to build up rules for the settlement of future differences between nations, just as the decisions of national courts make standards for administering justice between man and man.

Such, in briefest outline, were the achievements of the League and associated institutions. They are facts, easily to be confirmed in any impartial record of the last twenty-two years. They deserve not to be forgotten when opponents of supranational organization assert that the League accomplished nothing at all.

True, all these successes were not nearly enough to make a solid barrier against war. While they were being won, there were defeats in other quarters. We shall understand why the League failed in its big tests when we have examined the debit side of the ledger.

Poland claimed that Vilna rightly belonged to her, not to Lithuania, and took violent possession of the city. The Council of the League failed to bring about an impartial adjudication of the dispute and, despite the continued protests of Lithuania, allowed Poland to keep what she had taken. French influence in behalf of her protégé has been blamed for the Council's treatment of this case, as well as for the favor shown to Poland in the division of Upper Silesia between that country and Germany.

In 1923, Italian members of a Commission marking out the boundary between Albania and Greece were murdered at Janina in Greek territory. Italy demanded humiliating amends, including an indemnity of fifty million lire. The Greek Government rejected some of its demands, but declared its willingness to refer to the League and accept its decision. Italy replied by occupying Corfu, after a bombardment which killed fifteen and wounded more than thirty civilians. When Greece appealed to the Council at Geneva, Italy, herself a member of the Council, disputed the League's authority. The boundary commission was responsible to another body altogether, the Conference of Ambassadors at Paris, and that body alone must deal with the question. The Council agreed, though it might well have dealt with the seizure of Corfu as a breach of the Covenant; and the Conference of Ambassadors condemned Greece to satisfy the Italian demands. Thus again was the action of a strong and favored Power in taking the law into its own hands allowed to go unpunished and uncensured. It was unhappily not the last time that Mussolini would flaunt the Covenant.

Disagreements between its two greatest members had from the first been a major obstacle to the successful operation of the League. France, whose long land-frontier had been broken by two invasions in forty-four years and whose fields and cities had been ravaged by war, was never satisfied with the Covenant as a guaranty of her safety. At the Peace Conference she had wanted the left bank of the Rhine. This demand was dropped in return for a fifteen years' occupation of the left bank plus a draft treaty in which Great Britain and the United States jointly undertook to protect her against unprovoked aggression from Germany. The United States rejected this along with the Versailles Treaty. As the treaty was never intended to bind Britain separately, France was left without this reinforcement to her security. As an alternative she embarked on a program of alliances with Belgium, Poland, Czecho-Slovakia, Yugoslavia and Rumania. This was the policy of encirclement which was later to serve as one of Nazi Germany's chief complaints. Time after time the French tried to strengthen the Covenant and ensure prompt action by the League against an aggressor. That was the purpose of the Draft Treaty of Mutual Assistance, 1923, and of the Geneva Protocol, 1924. Both of these efforts were defeated by Great Britain with the active concurrence of the British Dominions. Far from strengthening the Covenant, the British nations seemed determined to weaken it.

The mutual guaranty of independence and territory contained in Article 10 had never held clear enough promise of practical measures to win French confidence. Canada, on the other hand, thought it much too precise, and had tried hard to get it deleted. Failing in this, the Dominion had submitted to the Assembly of 1923 a resolution that watered down an obligation already vague. True, the resolution fell short of unanimity by one vote; but no one doubted that it would be taken as deciding the meaning of the Article. Its effect was to give the constitutional authorities of each member the right to decide how far, if at all, the member would join in any military enforcement of the guaranty. This was like saying—"Yes, we promised to protect you, but you'll have to wait until our constitutional authorities have decided whether we're going to keep the promise. We hope your assailant will be polite enough to suspend operations while we deliberate."

At this time France seemed torn between two conflicting passions. Anxious to keep her historic enemy weak, she yet insisted on a scale of reparations which only a strong and prosperous nation could have begun to pay. In pursuit of both objectives, and assisted by Belgium, she had occupied the Ruhr, Germany's richest industrial area, in January, 1923. Britain stood aloof, neutral but censorious.

On paper, France showed a profit on the first year of occupation; but the invasion was followed by a sharp decline in the value of the franc and in the end it brought neither security nor economic advantage. Inflicting useless suffering and ruin on the Germans, it aggravated their hatred of the Versailles settlement, delayed European pacification for two years, antagonized opinion in Britain and elsewhere. By demonstrating the futility of repressive violence, it awakened a revulsion among the French themselves, and the government formed by Herriot after the defeat of Poincaré in 1924 was ready for a more co-operative policy.

With the Dawes Plan, which in August, 1924, revised the whole scheme of reparations, an era of reconciliation set in. Great Britain, though she rejected the general commitments of the Geneva Protocol, took a leading part in the negotiation of the narrowly limited Locarno Agreements. In these Great Britain and Italy guaranteed France and Belgium against attack by Germany, and Germany against attack by France or Belgium. Because they put her on the same footing as Germany, and because they contained no guaranty of the frontiers of her allies, France was never completely satisfied with this substitute for the Treaty of Mutual Guaranty or the Protocol. But Aristide Briand, her foreign minister, was resolved to make the best of it. With Austen Chamberlain of England and Gustav Stresemann of Germany he embarked on a program for Europe which now at last was imbued with a true spirit of co-operation. In September, 1926, Germany entered the League and took a permanent seat in the Council. A season of relative warmth brought forth the Briand plan for a United States of Europe. For a time it looked as if the problems of the "unruly continent" were on their way to general solution.

There was a bewildering variety of problems, quite enough to suggest the need of a Pan European organization for a concerted attack upon them. Political grievances vied for attention with economic maladjustments. Germans severed from the Fatherland at Danzig and Memel and in the Polish Corridor, Austrians and Hungarians under foreign rule in the Tyrol and along the Danube, were like a scattering of small volcanoes whose accumulating pressures constantly threatened eruption. The neighbors of Germany and Hungary accused those countries of secretly rearming for vengeance. Unemployment and hunger, ever present in Central and Eastern Europe since the war, were aggravated now by the monetary reform carried out in Germany after the great inflation of 1922 and 1923. Customs barriers and restrictions on imports and exports blocked the flow of international trade. The Economic Conference held at Geneva in 1927 drew up wise resolutions prescribing the cure for these evils, but no one followed the prescription.

Germany and Austria proposed to meet the most pressing of their economic needs by forming a customs union. This raised the specter of the *Anschluss*, that political fusion of the two countries which the Peace Treaties forbade and which France and her Danubian allies were determined to prevent. It brought to a frightened standstill the negotiations of 1929 and 1930 on Briand's project of European union. Then came the world-wide depression, and in the midst of it Japan's defiant invasion of Manchuria.

China appealed over and over again to the League, and once more the League failed to curb an arrogant aggressor. Great Britain, represented by Sir John Simon, felt too weak in the Pacific, too fearful of losing eastern markets, too uncertain of American reactions, to support any suggestion of sanctions. Canada and Australia shared her unwillingness. Collective security was again displayed as an empty formula. Coming on top of this confession of bankruptcy, the dismal and languishing failure of the two years' Disarmament Conference extinguished most of what hope still clung to the League as an instrument of joint political action.

Then, in 1935, came a chance to retrieve all that was lost. Italy, using the pretext of a border incident and after a pretense of arbitration, launched a long-planned invasion of Ethiopia. The Assembly of the League condemned the act as an aggression violating the Covenant, and fifty-one states joined in applying the economic and financial sanctions of Article 16. This looked like business.

Unhappily the leading members were again not firm in their purpose. France was half-hearted. It was only a few months since M. Laval, seeking aid against the rising power of Hitler, had gone to Rome with certain proposals for Mussolini's consideration. In return for a promise of consultation if Germany began rearming or attempted to absorb Austria, he agreed not to oppose an Italian demand for special concessions from Haile Selassie, Emperor of Ethiopia. The League's embarrassingly vigorous stand now placed the French Government in an awkward predicament. To refuse to join in sanctions after the Assembly's decision would have meant open repudiation of the Covenant. On the other hand, to assist in stopping the invasion would be to lose all the advantage gained at Rome and to throw Fascist Rome into the arms of Nazi Berlin. So France temporized.

Great Britain was less than whole-hearted. Italy was muttering threats of war, and Downing Street fairly shouted its assurances that it would not be drawn into hostilities to defend Ethiopia. Also there was fear that if Mussolini were exposed to failure in his military adventure, the Fascist regime might fall and be succeeded by Communism, the supreme evil in the eyes of British Tories. Sir Samuel Hoare, British Secretary of State for Foreign Affairs, made a plan with M. Laval to dismember Ethiopia and offer more than half the country to Italy. An outburst of popular indignation in England defeated this compromise; but care was nevertheless taken not to make the economic embargo too severe for the aggressor. The Canadian representative in the committee regulating sanctions had early in the proceedings raised the question of stopping oil shipments to Italy. His action was repudiated by Canada, which thus shares in the responsibility for the failure of the first sanctions experiment. For though it is doubtful whether the stoppage of oil could have prevented the actual conquest, which was far more rapid than anticipated, it might have served as a principal means of compelling Italy to make ultimate restitution.

Hitler had capitalized the Italian diversion and the want of resolution which it revealed in England and France. In March 1936 he violated the Treaty of Versailles and—what was more serious—the Locarno Agreements, by marching troops into the Rhineland. Convoked in London, the Council of the League declared the violation, but failed to advise any punitive or remedial action. The growing assertion of German power was ever an obstacle to effective action against Italy, and this latest defiance had much to do with the abandonment of sanctions in July 1936. France made desperate efforts to bolster up her crumbling security by new "Locarnos" for Eastern as well as Western Europe, but nothing came of her negotiations.

Four months after Germany remilitarized the Rhineland civil war broke out in Spain. Britain and France, terrified lest Russian aid to the Socialist Government of Spain and German-Italian aid to the Fascist rebels under Franco might plunge Europe into war, hurriedly arranged a non-intervention agreement binding twenty-four states. Moscow, Rome and Berlin were parties, but from all three came volunteers and equipment for Spain. In vain the Spanish Government called on the League to check what amounted in substance to an invasion by Italian and German forces. All that Geneva could produce was a declaration of the duty of all states not to intervene in the internal affairs of others. Franco, thanks to the superiority of his foreign support, established his dictatorship after two years of death and destruction; and a further victory rewarded the unchecked banditry of the Rome-Berlin Axis.

Then followed in rapid succession the invasion and absorption of Austria, the annexation of the Sudetenland without a serious attempt by any member of the League to fulfill Article 10 of the Covenant, the mockery of Munich with its unfulfilled promises to protect what was left of Czecho-Slovakia, the occupation of Memel and Danzig, the invasion of Poland, and at long last the English and French declarations of war in September 1939. Fearful and gullible, the British and French governments had gone from one surrender to another, always believing, apparently, that after the next gulp the aggressors would have enough. The small trickle of violence which they could easily have stopped by firm use of the League machinery a few years earlier, had become a flood. The direct menace to themselves could no longer be blinked.

For all of this disintegration the excuse is offered that England and France, in blind disregard of "realities," had disarmed. They had made the mistake, so the argument runs, of relying on pious hopes instead of on power. The answer to this is that the real error lay not in disarmament, but in disarmament accompanied by a policy of weakening and slighting the League. A nation can afford to disarm only if it is helping to build up a strong supranational community, just as men can go about unarmed only because they have made a state for their protection.

More serious is the contention that the League was doomed to failure from the moment that it was saddled with the duty of executing the Treaty of Versailles. For it can hardly be denied that the claims of that Treaty, disregarding as they did the principles of equity and flying in the face of economic reason, imposed a heavy burden of distrust and hatred on a new and struggling institution.

Here, as ever, the criticism is easier than the cure. Efforts to organize the human community are apt to follow great disruptions. The new institutions set up can hardly escape the task of reconstruction and restitution. It will be wise to separate the conference which settles the immediate terms of peace from that which lays down a constitution for the future. Passions may cool in the interval; and the inclusion in the second conference of states relatively unaffected by hostilities may bring calmer judgment to bear on long-term problems. Nevertheless, the immediate conditions of peace will themselves have to be imbued with the spirit of the final organization, and the final organization must make ample provision for periodic readjustment. No static order will suffice; life is essentially dynamic, and surely we have learnt enough to know that a fortified *status quo* means not peace but explosive fermentation.

What now of the argument so often heard that the League might as well have folded up when the United States refused to come in? Certainly that decision meant that the organization could no longer count on the great predominance of power which had been assumed by its founders. Perhaps, again, the United States might have supplied the courageous and far-sighted leadership which was so woefully lacking. But at crucial points, such as the Manchurian issue, the disarmament conference, the fiasco of sanctions against Italy, there was so much evidence of other considerations at work that we must continue to doubt whether the Covenant would have been fulfilled even if the United States had been a member. Narrow views of national interest, and the skepticism of important governments as to the validity of the whole idea of supranational community, might have defeated even a strong American initiative. Sometimes, it seems, the absence of the United States was not so much a factor preventing success as a ready excuse for not taking action which the principal governments did not wish to take.

While no invitation from without or pressure from within had been sufficient to bring the United States into the League, that country did not remain altogether aloof from the peace effort of the 'twenties. It was on the initiative of President Harding's administration that the Washington Disarmament Conference was held in 1921. The treaties concluded there temporarily averted a race in naval building and held in check for ten years the ambitions of Japan on the Asiatic mainland. Battleship tonnage for the United States, the British Commonwealth, Japan, France and Italy was limited to a scale of percentages, in the order given, of 100, 100, 60, 35 and 35. The construction of naval bases or new fortifications within a specified portion of the Pacific area was prohibited. These agreements were the most effective measure yet taken to curb the accumulation of armaments with its economic cost and its threat to peace.

The Washington Treaty did not limit the building of cruisers and lighter naval craft. But it did scrap some British and American battleships and suspend further building in this class. That fact, along with the dropping of the Anglo-Japanese Alliance, is held by the advocates of peace-by-armament to have been the main cause of the subsequent failure to restrain Japanese aggression in the Western Pacific. The United States and Great Britain, upon whom must fall the task of control, had, it is argued, given up both the political advantage and the physical power necessary for the enterprise.

Certainly the lack of a powerful fleet in Eastern waters was one of the excuses offered by Great Britain for not keeping her word when Japan invaded Manchuria. Whether, in view of the economic crisis, she would have taken action even with a preponderant force on the spot, must remain one of the gratuitous speculations of history. It is no speculation, but a fact, that the Washington agreements of nonaggression in the Pacific were allowed, like the Covenant of the League, to die of neglect. With them passed away naval limitation. The fate of the whole scheme is another demonstration of the weakness of unco-ordinated effort directed from different centers. The divided, halting and overlapping operation of the Nine Power arrangement on the one side and the League of Nations on the other, while Japan, defying both the Covenant and the Washington Treaties, took forceful possession of Chinese territory, was a spectacle of tragic confusion in the face of a great need and a great opportunity.

The Nine Power Treaty or Pact was one of several agreements which were at once the condition and the completion of the naval limitation treaty. In a Four Power Treaty, the United States, the British Empire, France and Japan agreed to respect their rights in relation to their insular possessions and dominions in the Pacific and to consult together if any dispute arose between them about those rights or if any other Power should threaten them. In the Nine Power Treaty the United States, the British Empire, Japan, France, Italy, the Netherlands, Belgium, and Portugal agreed with China to respect the sovereignty, independence and territorial and administrative integrity of China, to establish and maintain equal opportunity for the commerce of all nations in Chinese territory, to assist in the achievement of stable government over the country, and to seek no special rights or privileges there which would curtail those of the nationals of other states. The Four Power Treaty brought with it the termination of the Anglo-Japanese Alliance, never popular in the United States. The Nine Power Treaty was thought to usher in a new era of security and peaceful progress for China. Its consultation clause was considered sufficient guaranty that any conflict between foreign interests in that country would be settled without violence.

The Nine Power Treaty set up no tribunal for the adjudication of disputes and, though it provided for consultation, imposed no obligation of joint or several action against any nation violating its principles. With these defects, and because it was accompanied by no arrangement to meet the growing economic need of Japan, it simply melted away before the Island Empire's determination to achieve its purposes by its own means. The United States invoked it without avail when the great depression of the 'thirties unnerved the western democracies to the point of nonresistance and, while sharpening Japan's need, simultaneously opened the way for her expansion.

Equally ineffective was the Pact of Paris, originally proposed by M. Aristide Briand, French Minister for Foreign Affairs, taken up by Mr. Kellogg, United States Secretary of State, and, after signature at Paris on August 27, 1928, eventually accepted by no less than sixty-five states.

In this treaty, otherwise known as the Briand-Kellogg Pact, the nations of the world condemned recourse to war for the solution of international controversies and renounced war as an instrument of national policy. They likewise agreed never to seek by other than peaceful means the settlement of any dispute, whatever its nature, that might arise between them. But the text contained no arrangement for the adjudication of disputes and no sanction for the violation of its obligations. Depending wholly on conscience and "the public opinion of mankind" for its effect, it proved no deterrent to Japan's invasion of China, Italy's conquest of Ethiopia, or Germany's seizure of Czecho-Slovakia. Under the Stimson doctrine of nonrecognition, the United States has consistently refused to recognize the validity of territorial acquisitions made in contravention of its terms; but this assertion of the survival and legal vigor of the Pact has not increased its efficacy as an instrument of peace and justice.

The structure of the international community was like an arch built by different hands at different times and without a keystone. Came the strain which each section had been intended to resist, and not one part but the whole crumbled in ruin.

The peace plans of the 'twenties failed to keep the peace. Are we to conclude that such planning is useless? Perhaps the plans were thrown together in too much of a hurry and with too little understanding of what they meant. Many people thought so from the beginning and offered us carefully studied alternatives. Possibly these constructive criticisms, coupled with the experience we have had, may point the way to a better job in the future.

CHAPTER III

GRAND DESIGNS

In the seventeenth century the Duc de Sully, one time French Superintendent of Finance, set out in his Memoirs a great plan of European organization which he pretended to have devised with his royal master, Henry IV. Europe was to be divided between fifteen states, grouped under six regional councils and one general council. The regional councils were to be so situated and so equipped with authority and power as to compel the settlement of disputes in their regions, while the general council was to concern itself with wars and other enterprises in which the whole "universal and very Christian republic" was concerned.

This project, attributed by its author partly to the French king, has always been known as "The Grand Design of Henry IV." It combines regional and general organization in much the same way as many plans produced in our own day. Another modern touch is that Sully considers Russia too barbarous for inclusion in his "universal and very Christian republic." Because of the eminence of the authors, real and alleged, this design has been one of the most familiar. But both in Sully's age and much earlier there were many projects of European or world union whose detail resembles most surprisingly that of the League Covenant or drafts to improve the Covenant. For centuries thoughtful men have sought peace, and in their search have drafted great commonwealths that won the intellectual admiration of their fellows.

None of these grand designs was put into practice. International unions and bureaus for particular purposes such as communications by post and telegraph were set up in the nineteenth century; but it was not until 1919, after the First World War, that the nations actually joined in a general society for the orderly conduct of international relations.

The Covenant to which they then subscribed bore detailed resemblance to some of the long line of unrealized projects reaching back to the Renaissance—evidence that even the disregarded thought of the study may have a part in determining the shape of things to come.

Even in the first and best years of the League of 1919, there were many Europeans whose passionate desire for security was not satisfied. Not only did successive French governments press for supplementary guaranties, but unofficial groups sprang up to urge closer and stronger union.

In 1922, Count Coudenhove-Kalergi founded at Vienna an association devoted to the cause of Pan European Union. This movement enlisted the support of active politicians as well as private citizens in a number of countries, particularly in France. M. Aristide Briand was an Honorary President, and in 1925 M. Herriot, then Prime Minister, gave the association his approval in the *Chambre*. From its present headquarters in Berne, it still continues its work, and the founder publishes books and articles and delivers lectures in Europe and America. His crusade may well produce important results in the future. It is already of some historical significance, for it clearly had much to do with M. Briand's initiative when, in 1929, he laid before the League of Nations the proposals for a United States of Europe which have ever since been associated with his name.

The *Memorandum on the Organization of a System of European Federal Union*, which was circulated by M. Briand in May 1930, after preliminary discussion at the 1929 Assembly of the League, is a curious mixture of draft constitution and mere suggestions to be worked out by a proposed series of constituent conferences. It speaks of "future Federal Union," "the European Commonwealth," "the European Union," "a close and permanent pacific union." It advocates a European Conference composed of representatives of all the European Members of the League of Nations to act as "the primary directing body," and an executive body consisting of a certain number only of the members of the European Conference. But it leaves the powers, the exact composition, the organization, and the procedure of these bodies to be settled by future meetings of the states of Europe.

Two features of the *Memorandum* have already the ring of an old-fashioned conservatism. These are the careful reservation of the "independence and national sovereignty of each state," and "the general subordination of the economic problem to the political problem." Later plans of union start from the axiom that the sovereignty of the state is a dangerous myth, and recognize that the interweaving of politics and economics in the modern world make the regulation of economic relations an essential function of any future organization for the preservation of peace.

M. Briand contemplated "the general development in Europe of the system of arbitration and security and the progressive extension to the whole European commonwealth of the policy of international guarantees inaugurated at Locarno, culminating in the fusion of special agreements or series of special agreements into a more comprehensive system." This was his closest approach to any mechanism for the compulsory settlement of disputes and the enforcement of federal decisions, whether legislative, executive or judicial. There is no specific mention in his memorandum of that commonplace of subsequent planners, peaceful change—the adjustment without violence of situations which, while they correspond to existing law, impose inequitable hardship. Clearly the Briand sketch, which attracted so much attention for a year or two, evaded or postponed the principal difficulties involved in the creation of an efficient wider community.

Of the European governments invited to comment on M. Briand's memorandum, a few were enthusiastic, many cautious, some critical. The discussion was continued into the 1930 Assembly of the League, which referred the matter to a Commission of Inquiry for European Union, consisting of representatives of all the European states members of the League. This body was reasonably diligent for some time, but the project of union was ultimately lost in a series of more engrossing developments beginning with the Austro-German proposals for a customs union, and carrying on through the dreary labyrinths of the Disarmament Conference into the catastrophes of the great depression.

Much of the vagueness of this draft for a closer association of the states of Europe is to be accounted for by the desire of the French Government of that date to keep the proposed union strictly "within the framework of the League of Nations." The omission of Russia and Turkey is to be attributed to the fact that these countries were not yet League members. In a very real sense, the United States of Europe was to be a Committee of the League for European affairs. This intention is made evident by many provisions linking the two institutions, among others by the enumeration among the Union's functions of "the special measures to be taken to accelerate the execution by the European governments of the general decisions of the League of Nations." Its value must be assessed against the background of the League as it was in 1930. In that setting it escapes the reproach of many contemporary plans, namely that they appear to assume that the total problem of peace can be solved by the rational organization of Europe, and of a Europe, at that, which excludes the Soviet Union.

Having come from the study to the council table, the plan for a united Europe was driven by the swift rush of threatening events back into the study again. There it has received further elaboration, has taken on new forms and, in some hands, been extended to include all the democracies and eventually the world. Lionel Curtis in his *Civitas Dei*, Clarence Streit in his *Union Now*, have rung the changes on the federal theme. The histories of the United States, Switzerland, and Canada have been drawn into service to show how competing autonomies can be reconciled by the division of functions and powers between a central, federated government and the governments of the federated states or provinces. With scant acknowledgment to earlier thinkers, Alexander Hamilton and his *Federalist* have been brought from the archives of the American revolutionary period and refurbished into the prophet and the gospel of a new world order. Amidst some fanaticism, much valuable work has been done in revealing the weaknesses of existing international organization and in devising complete constitutional forms for alternative modes of association. We shall return in a later chapter to the study of federalism as a possible solution of the problem of war and peace. Our present purpose is a preliminary general survey of the different types of proposal now circulating in relation to this problem.

The creation of one great state embracing all of the world's political communities in a union as intimate as that existing between the states of the United States of America, the provinces of Canada or the cantons of Switzerland, while it may be the end toward which man is moving, is commonly regarded as too difficult an ideal to be realized in any measurable future. Yet the proposition that some form of universal association, wielding effective authority over certain branches of human activity, is not only desirable but a necessary condition of peace, finds strong support among politicians and political scientists alike. Rough sketches of such an association have been offered by statesmen in official pronouncements, and more or less exact "blueprints" have been drafted by scholars. These are being circulated among groups in different countries and are undergoing an examination quite without precedent in distribution and intensity.

Most of this thought refuses to jettison associations already tried and found partially successful. Most of it retains, for example, parts of the machinery of the League of Nations. In the main, however, it rejects the idea of a single association which would employ the same institutions for the solution of problems which are essentially regional as for those which transcend regional boundaries. There is a marked tendency, for instance, to conclude from the experience of the League that military sanctions, if and when they become necessary, should be the business of regional associations. Some thinkers boldly advocate a world police force of military, naval and air units, strong enough to overcome aggression anywhere; but even they are inclined to treat this as a desirable future development rather than an immediate part of their post-war organization.

Among existing associations integrated in these drafts of universal community is the Pan American system. It is accepted as axiomatic that the United States must be a leading member of any future world society of nations. In any circumstances, after the present war, which will permit resumption of the democratic organization for peace, the relative position of that republic will be infinitely stronger than it was in 1919, and the need for its full co-operation proportionately greater. Recent progress in the consolidation of the inter-American community, combined with the long tradition of special responsibility in the western hemisphere, makes it probable that Washington will be more sympathetic to an organization recognizing and incorporating this regional association as a unit than to one breaking it up into its component states. Naturally the views of the Latin-American nations will be of the first importance, but the pre-war trend away from the League is some indication that their policy would take the same direction.

The Pacific too is thought likely to require an association of its own, and the model commonly accepted is the Nine Power Pact. This time, however, Russia would be a necessary party, and Australia, New Zealand, and probably Canada, would assume distinct membership in what Raymond Leslie Buell calls a "Pacific Conference." Like many other commenators, Buell recommends in his *Isolated America* that the Pact be strengthened by establishing a Pacific tribunal for regional disputes and by an arrangement for sanctions against a violator of its provisions.

For Europe a variety of solutions is offered, all of them federal in character, but ranging from a single union for the whole continent to a series of three or more federations grouping the states according to geographic contiguity and economic interdependence. These multi-federal plans adopt a principle of sub-regionalism for Europe, and a question still requiring study is whether the several groups so formed should be linked in an all-European association of their own, which would be integrated as a unit in the world society of states, or should come directly under that society. It is of course fantastic to suppose that so complex an organization could be completed at one stroke. The essential thing is to begin with a framework sufficiently strong to secure peace and co-operation, yet sufficiently flexible to permit progressive development. The chance of making such a beginning when the time comes to rebuild will depend largely upon the amount of consideration given in the meantime to the various forms of association which are hypothetically possible.

The regionalist school—if we may so characterize those who advocate an interlocking association of groups of states rather than a single league or union—looks upon the Soviet Union as a regional group by itself, to be co-ordinated with the others in the world society. This solution to the problem of finding the right place for a Power which is European (to an increasingly important degree in recent months) as well as Asiatic, is sketched by Buell in the book already cited, and by Julian Huxley in the paper entitled "Science, War and Reconstruction," in *Science*, New York, February 15, 1940. Too many of the projects devoted exclusively or mainly to European union cast the Soviets in the role of public enemy number one and direct their organization against the Kremlin and all its works. Thus, like all plans built upon a principle of defensive exclusiveness rather than progressive co-operation, they doom themselves to ultimate collapse.

A new feature of present thought on world organization is the consideration given to economic needs and forces. The lesson of the treaties of 1919, with the disastrous consequences that followed the severance of territories irrevocably interdependent and the imposition of crushing financial burdens upon communities deprived of the means of carrying them, is still vividly present in the academic, if not in the public, mind. Hence the elaborate studies of an economic organization which will not only assist in the difficult transition from an economy of war to one of peace, but guarantee the distribution of essential food and raw materials and prevent the rise of barriers to trade. Here again the partially successful institutions of the last two decades are re-established and reinforced. The cartel system is taken over from the great private industries that operate over national boundaries and, with government and consumer representation in the directing boards, made subject to the general supervision of a world trade commission. The Bank of International Settlements is expanded into a world central bank and given the task of stabilizing currencies. Through subsidiaries or co-ordinate institutions it would control international investment and provide financing for the development of needy areas. The restored economic and financial sections of the League would assist these organs with research and expert advice.

Closely co-ordinated with the economic machinery would be a strengthened establishment to direct a universal attack upon social problems. Working with the restored Health and Social sections of the League, the International Labor Organization and a new Committee on Migration and Settlement would concern themselves with the immediate and pressing problem of the world's refugees and with a long-term program of improvement of labor, housing and sanitary conditions. The resources of material and energy now poured into destruction would be diverted into channels of construction and progress.

As a concrete example of the best type of inquiry and suggestion along these lines there follows a summary of a plan worked out by a group of private persons in England. The work was done before the collapse of France and, like so many essays of that period, it begins with the assumption of an Anglo-French victory and with the Anglo-French union for war purposes as a nucleus of permanent organization for peace. Some of its apparent value would therefore be gone if it had to be regarded as a precise program for post-war action. Yet the general directives laid down retain all of their validity and may still be considered the essential elements of democratic as opposed to despotic world government.

The central problem is Europe. One of the League's weaknesses was that it attempted to achieve European and world order in a single unitary organization. Europe requires its own supranational authority, and the nucleus of this must be found in the perpetuation of the Anglo-French union.

Between armistice and treaty the allied army, assisted by its contingents from the Dominions and from the states overrun by Nazi Germany, must keep order and guarantee security against any recrudescence of militarism. This immediate task may indeed extend for some time beyond the treaty; but with the addition of other states to the Anglo-French nucleus the military force will become more broadly representative and will evolve into the overwhelmingly powerful police agency which the League lacked and which is a prime essential of lasting peace.

The Northern and Western democracies of Europe, and even many states of the Balkan and Mediterranean areas, would quickly realize an identity of interest with the inchoate federation and desire to be included in it. The already existing tendency to a grouping of these smaller states into Northern, Danubian and Near Eastern federations should be encouraged, for the larger composite units so formed would be less susceptible to domination by the Great Powers and would thus be better able not only to advance the just interests of their regions but to ensure the general European direction of the central federation.

It is believed that the suppression of militaristic forces in Germany, coupled with the growth of a quasi-federal association powerful enough to preserve order in Europe and devoted at the same time to increasing the welfare of all Europeans, would enable the more liberal elements of the German people to get and hold control in their country. Under such control Germany would become an active partner in a scheme of co-operation that would provide full scope for the special gifts of its population.

The Soviet Union is left out of the developing federation of Europe, though not quite out of the calculations of the authors of this plan. The exclusion is explained by the statement that Russia is in reality a federal system by itself, differing in culture and political tradition from the West. The authors believe that the federalization of Europe will create the conditions for a more stable and more benevolent balance between the Soviets and their Western neighbors. It is hoped, moreover (and to many readers the hope will appear justified by the conduct of the Soviets in the League), that the Union of Soviet Republics may be a willing participant in the wider scheme of world organization which the group sketches as a setting for its federation of Europe.

Italy, having joined with Germany in the war, is to be treated in the same way as her ally.

In keeping with their view that the federalization of Europe must necessarily be a gradual process dependent on the growing sense of community and of the utility of common organization, the authors refrain from laying down a detailed and fixed constitution. To begin with, a European Council consisting of the premiers and leading ministers of the participating states will be necessary. This is one of the points where the march of events has demolished part of the material with which the authors worked. The Supreme Council co-ordinating the war effort of France and Great Britain was to serve as the nucleus of this body, representatives of other states being added as they joined the association.

Under the European Council, it might be desirable to establish a general European Assembly representing directly the peoples according to their geographical or functional distribution. The immediate purpose of this body would be to provide a place for the discussion of grievances, the general determination of policy and supervision of expenditure; but it might develop in time the legislative and other powers of a parliament.

Two technical bodies are to operate under the control of the Council, a European police agency and an agency for social and economic reconstruction and development.

The first task of the police agency would be to command the Allied Force, expanded by contingents from other states as indicated above, in its mission of maintaining order, securing the disarmament of Germany and preventing militaristic elements from regaining power. During this period, little progress toward general European disarmament is to be expected, but that objective is never to be lost sight of and every measure consistent with security is to be taken to prepare the way for its achievement.

Disarmament is the stage at which this study passes over from its scheme of European federalization to one of world order. The problem is dealt with in terms of world control of armaments and world police. Heavy tanks and heavy artillery are to be forbidden to individual states, along with military aircraft. A control commission is to examine at intervals the position in each participating state, and automatic economic sanctions are to fall upon any offender. International land forces regionally organized and controlled, and strong in the weapons forbidden to states, are to be distributed in strategic places from which they can dominate nations likely to be dangerous.

There are to be two naval zones. The Pacific and Western Atlantic are to be policed by an international navy to which the United States will be the chief contributor, the remaining seas by a similar force in which British and French units will play the largest part. In each zone the international navy is to have the sole right to maintain warships of any sort and is to control all bases. The two forces would be maintained at an agreed ratio and part of their duty would be to stop the seaborne commerce of any state declared an aggressor by competent international authority.

Air forces are to be distributed so as to co-operate both with the land forces and with the two navies.

The economic and social agency operating under the European Council is to have at its disposal a budget of perhaps a hundred million pounds sterling per annum. This money is to be spent partly on European development in the fields of communication, education, research, health, and credit facilities, and partly on large-scale enterprises in the colonies.

The mandate system is extended to all colonial dependencies of European states, the Mandates Commission of the League is strengthened by giving it powers of investigation on the spot, and the principle of trusteeship is recognized. While leaving to the League the responsibility for the system in general, the authors create a Colonial Commission under their European Council to supervise the government of colonies mandated to European states and to administer grants to such colonies from the European budget. They allow the existing colonial Powers to carry on local administration, but provide for the internationalization even of this function by throwing open the colonial services of these Powers to a proportion of foreigners.

To the central authorities of the European association are to be assigned far more extensive duties and powers in the control of production, distribution of commodities, and provision of credit, than have hitherto been placed in the hands of any supranational body. Existing cartels are to be used as the starting-point of new development, but the selfish and restrictionist tactics of these organs are to be transformed to the service of the world-community by the addition of government and consumer representation to their boards of control and by making them responsible to a Permanent Cartel Commission. International Public Concerns are to undertake the production of essential commodities in backward colonial areas, and a body is to be established for the issue of rural loans for agricultural improvements in countries not possessing adequate financial resources for such development.

For the settlement of "justiciable disputes" (defined as those "concerning questions of existing right and of fact") the authors are content with the Permanent Court of International Justice, which is strengthened by making its jurisdiction in such matters compulsory. As for disputes which can only be disposed of finally by a change in existing legal rights, they hold that these fall outside the natural competence of judicial organs, but hesitate to refer them to any of the international authorities which they propose to set up. This part of the work is surprisingly weak, for it drops the difficult problem of peaceful change back into the laps of the governments which have in the past distinguished themselves chiefly by their failure to solve it.

In the past there has been a wide gap between those who plan for social justice within the state community and those who plan for peace and justice between states. The socialist has been inclined to despise projects of co-operation between nations as hopelessly futile until socialism has been adopted as the universal doctrine of government, while the internationalist has usually been content to construct the machinery of interstate co-operation and leave the welfare of the individual to autonomous agencies of the state. The establishment of the International Labor Organization and its association with the League of Nations was some recognition of the interconnection between these two lines of endeavor; but the forces which destroyed the League demonstrated the necessity of a far closer integration of economic, social and political activities on the international plane. The plan summarized here has the great merit of recognizing that international organization and internal social progress must proceed *pari passu*.

The authors, like H. G. Wells in his *New World Order*, draft a bill of universal human rights, though in much briefer form. The essentials are freedom of thought, expression and movement; the national and international rule of law; the use of the state not merely as an instrument of domination, police and protection of private interests, but for public welfare and cultural development; and, finally, the ordering of production and distribution so as to improve conditions of living everywhere. Unlike Mr. Wells, the authors of our plan construct an international organization in which these ends might be achieved.

With all its excellences, however, their work leaves aside one large and essential element in the organization of peace for Europe. It touches on the Pacific area in its admirable arrangements for the colonies and again in its disposition of the naval police forces; but it nowhere defines even in broadest outline a form of association for the Pacific Powers. True, the authors explicitly state their conviction that the first step toward world peace must be to set the European house in order. But unregulated competition for markets and influence in the Far East, and the resulting special relationships set up between European and Eastern Powers, will not cease to be disturbing elements in the European household itself. Trade and finance, colonial security and colonial development, the sanitary and social conditions of populations, migration, the settlement of inevitable disputes, all of these will demand stable arrangement involving not merely the European, but also the American and Asiatic states, as active partners. The validity of a plan of peaceful collaboration in Europe cannot in other words be estimated in European terms alone; whether it can operate will depend in no small measure upon the question how it works out in the Far East. The reader cannot but regret the failure of so competent a group to apply this test.

The prominent features of the plan just summarized recur again and again in books and articles written in England, France, Switzerland, the United States and Australia. References to the widespread literature growing up around the subject will be found in the following pages. With the conquest of France and subsequent developments in the war, emphasis has shifted from the Anglo-French union to Anglo-American collaboration as the nucleus and driving power for future world organization. Yet in its broad lines the work of this English group still finds much support as a statement of the ultimate objectives of American and British policy.

CHAPTER IV

ASCENDANCY OF THE FEDERAL IDEA

With some reverses, the idea of federalism as the means whereby man may rise from his present chaos into an ordered world has been gathering strength since the early twenties of this century. One high point was reached when, as we have seen, M. Briand's plan for a United States of Europe became the subject of official discussion in the League of Nations between 1929 and 1931. After this the idea suffered an eclipse from which it gradually emerged as the League fell into its decline and the drift toward a new war became a race for alliances and armaments. Out of this period of gathering storm came two leading books—*Civitas Dei* by Lionel Curtis, who had spent much of his life building constitutions in the British Commonwealth, and *Union Now* by Clarence Streit, an American correspondent at Geneva who had watched at close hand the crumbling of the League.

From a broad survey of political history, Curtis draws the conclusion that the self-governing commonwealth is the product of man's innate desire to serve his fellows. In the satisfaction of this desire he has learnt to curb his selfish wishes in the interest of his community. But so long as the sense of duty is limited to people of the same race, we cannot have peace in the world. Human nature will realize its full possibilities only with the achievement of a commonwealth coterminous with human society.

Our present civilization is due to the development of national commonwealths. But it is stopped from further progress by the belief that the nation-state is the ultimate in social organization. The League of Nations was not enough. It failed in its mission of world peace because the states members were allowed to retain their sovereignty and the exclusive title to the loyalty of their nationals. This is of the essence of a mere league, which therefore, while it may do useful work as a mechanism of voluntary co-operation, can never be molded into a real world government. World government must have all the power necessary to deal with the issues of peace and war. Such power and authority can be drawn not from a compact between independent states, but only from their citizens, whose loyalty to the world community must transcend any local allegiance.

Political wisdom and virtue have in the past been developed, more than by anything else, by the actual creation and operation of free institutions and the practice of self-government. So, too, the world can best be taught the possibility and the advantages of fusion into one community by demonstration on a limited scale. The first practical step toward the formation of a world-commonwealth would be the union of a small number of now independent states into one state. The best material with which to begin will be states with the same language, similar institutions, and long practice in the art of self-government. Curtis selects Great Britain, Australia and New Zealand. The citizens of these countries would most easily develop and demonstrate loyalty to an entity wider than the nation-state, and thus bridge the gap in men's minds between the state as it now is and the world-commonwealth of the future.

This federation of three would have a joint legislature and executive which would impose and collect taxes for federal purposes, operating always upon the individual citizen. Voting and tax-paying for two generations would engender devotion. The federation would find its first common interest in the maintenance of the routes between its units, and in time it might be joined by other countries vitally interested in these routes, such as Egypt, India, Holland. Later would come Belgium and the Scandinavian countries. In this expansion the most difficult step would be the inclusion of the first non-British state. Progress from that point would be easier and more rapid. Thus the British Commonwealth would complete its work as a stage in the long process of political integration which moves toward universal human community in the *Civitas Dei*, the Commonwealth of God.

The main thesis of Streit's well-known book is the same as that of Curtis in *Civitas Dei*. Neither writer sees any hope of peace in a mere league of nations which preserves intact the sovereignty of its states members, which acts only by unanimous decision and even then must depend for action upon forces which remain under control of the states, which has no supreme tribunal with compulsory jurisdiction and no legislature competent to adapt the law to changing conditions, which exercises no authority over the individual citizen and makes no appeal to his loyalty.

In other respects, the two books are very different. Streit proposes at once a much larger federation than Curtis dares to suggest as a beginning, and goes into details of organization which Curtis leaves entirely to others.

Union Now, published before the outbreak of war in 1939, urges the immediate federation of fifteen democracies, Australia, Belgium, Canada, Denmark, Finland, France, Ireland, Netherlands, New Zealand, Norway, Sweden, Union of South Africa, Great Britain, United States, and Switzerland. Only democracies are chosen because the preservation and increase of man's freedom is the prime objective of world government, and totalitarianism, which rejects that principle of democracy, cannot co-operate in its realization. Futhermore, it is Streit's belief that world government cannot be established by states as entities but only by the individuals in the states. This means participation in, and loyalty to, an organization over and above the state, features which are contrary to the essential philosophy of dictatorship. The author accordingly makes it a condition of the subsequent admission of other states that they shall have adopted democratic forms of government. The choice of democracies mentioned is determined by their combination of great power, strong existing bonds of community, and mature political experience. The Union would be militarily invulnerable, economically rich and financially stable. Its peoples would have complete security at much less cost than their present imperfect defenses, and this relief from the dead burden of armaments, combined with the removal of trade barriers, would raise the standard of living to heights never yet attained.

The government of the Union is to have power in those matters in which common administration will best serve man's freedom. Such matters would include citizenship, defense, trade, currency, postal and other communications. All matters in which freedom can best be served by local administration are to be left to the national governments. This distribution of powers, according to Streit, would guarantee the freedom of each federated state to experiment politically, economically and socially.

At this point the reader will be well advised to ponder a criticism of Mr. Wells in his *New World Order*, to the effect that money can only be kept common between communities adopting the same principles of economic organization. It would probably also be impossible to maintain free trade and a common currency between political units following divergent social policies, for these would almost inevitably involve profound differences in economic practice. The history of federations is against the view that they could tolerate profound social and economic differences, witness the underlying causes of the Civil War in the United States.

The Union is to have the power to tax the people directly, for it cannot be left to depend on state contributions; must raise and command its own armed forces, have its own machinery of law enforcement, and must enact laws bearing directly upon the citizen, not simply upon the federated state.

The federal organs of the Union are a bicameral Legislature, an executive Board, a Prime Minister and Cabinet, and a High Court.

The House of Deputies is elected by the people of the federated democracies, that is to say by the citizens of the Union, one deputy for every million of population. This gives the United States 129 deputies, Great Britain 47, France 42, Canada 11, the Netherlands 8, and Australia 7, to mention the half-dozen states with the largest représentation. In the Senate there is a minimum representation of each state by two, with an additional two Senators for every twenty-five million of population after the first twenty-five. The United States would thus have ten Senators, Great Britain and France four each, and all the other members two each.

The Board consists of five persons, three elected directly by the citizens of the Union, one by the House of Deputies and one by the Senate. These persons are, in rotation, Presidents of the Board. It is commander-in-chief of the armed forces of the Union, appoints diplomatic agents and consuls, makes treaties with the assent of Congress (the House and Senate) and the Premier.

The Premier is appointed by the Board, which delegates to him all the executive powers not expressly retained by it in this Constitution. He is assisted by a Cabinet of his own choice and remains in office so long as he retains the confidence of Congress.

The High Court, whose judges are appointed for life to a number not less than eleven, has jurisdiction in all controversies between states of the Union, between the citizens of different states, between a state and citizens of another state, and between states or citizens of the Union and foreign states.

Streit devotes part of his book to the effort to persuade his fellow Americans that the Union which he plans is urgently necessary for the United States. It is safe to say that when he wrote the majority of his countrymen would have refused to follow him into this close association with the warring states of Europe. Nor is there yet clear evidence that the successes of totalitarian arms and diplomacy have so changed the American mind that this type of project, even though restricted in immediate scope to the English-speaking nations, as in his later works Streit restricts it,[1] would be acceptable to it. Even if the people of the United States were willing to make this drastic break with their tradition of aloofness, there would be a strong resistance in Europe to many features of the Constitution. Representation by population, for instance, though it is a principle difficult to reject, would probably be unpalatable to Englishmen and Frenchmen with their forty-seven and forty-two deputies respectively, in the Federal House, against one hundred and twenty-nine from the United States. If the people themselves could be persuaded to accept what would look like government by the United States (though in fact the American deputies would represent their countrymen and not their country) their political leaders would almost certainly be too bitterly opposed to such a sacrifice of their present power and prestige to give the electorates a chance to express their will in the matter.

Another serious objection, based this time on the desirability rather than the practicability of Streit's plan, is that by its exclusion of the totalitarian states it would sharpen and perpetuate the division of the world into democracies and dictatorships. The opposition set up would hardly be mitigated by the standing invitation to adopt democratic forms of government and join the Union. On the contrary, the tendency in the totalitarian states would be to draw more closely together and to compete for the adherence of unattached political units. Thus the world would still be divided into armed camps juggling an unstable balance of power.

Curtis and Streit found many devoted disciples and more partial adherents. Numbers of commentators accepted the principles laid down in the two books, but rejected both plans of execution and concentrated on advocacy of the federal union of European states. The outbreak of war in September 1939 only increased the volume of oral and written support for such projects.

Nor was this merely the work of irresponsible enthusiasts. Politicians and public officials, even political parties,

[1] See, e.g., *Union Now with Britain*, 1941.

aligned themselves with the movement. British and French cabinet ministers spoke of the wartime association of Britain and France as the beginning of a permanent union which would form the nucleus of general federalization in Europe. Businessmen, civil servants, economists and lawyers set themselves singly or in groups to the task of working out in detail the constitutional forms necessary to carry these proposals into effect. The Parliamentary Labor Party in Great Britain dedicated itself to the establishment of a new commonwealth of states whose collective authority must transcend, within its proper sphere, the sovereign rights of separate states. It became a commonplace in England that the present war must clear the way for "some kind of federal union in Europe."

This sudden tide of interest in constitution-making for a working community of Europe is a curious reversal of British habit and tradition. For themselves the English have avoided anything in the nature of a fixed fundamental law determining, in a logically ordered text, the functions and powers of the various agencies of their national society. They have preferred to "broaden down from precedent to precedent" or—less poetically—to muddle through. Their policy in the League of Nations had about it always an air of regret at having committed themselves to so many *a priori* obligations, and their characteristic distaste for present undertakings to act in hypothetical future situations was exemplified by their rejection of the Geneva Protocol of 1924 and subsequent French proposals for an international military establishment.

The rise of Hitler, and the inability of France and England to circumvent his designs by diplomacy and alliance, destroyed the last shreds of "splendid isolation" in the British Isles. The government itself offered France a constitutional union, and everywhere among the people there developed a new willingness to contemplate participation in a close-knit European polity. Books, articles, pamphlets, privately circulated memoranda, carried endorsement of the principle and blueprints for its application.

Reference has already been made to Harold Nicolson's *Why Britain Is at War.* The last chapter of that essay contains a sketch of European federation, and the author returns to the charge in *The New Republic* for February 20, 1940. An interesting feature of this article is his statement that the vast majority of people in Great Britain believe that the establishment of a new world order must begin with federation in Europe. A bulky volume of speeches and writing supports this contention.

One question of special concern to the English writers is the effect of Britain's entry into a European union upon the bonds uniting the Commonwealth. Must the Dominions also be brought in? Desirable but not essential, says Sir William Beveridge in his paper, *Peace by Federation.* So important, says W. Ivor Jennings in his painstaking book, *A Federation for Western Europe,* that in order to induce them to accept membership the other members should be prepared to grant them special privileges and limited liability. Mr. Jennings, writing from an unconcealed British point of view, starts from the assumption that the British nations would in no circumstances consent to breaking up their present association. His concessions to this presumed passion of cohesion would be the signal for a host of reservations of special interests by other states. An alternative more conducive to general acceptance would be to leave the ties of Commonwealth (which have historically proved themselves sufficiently elastic to accommodate the most anomalous developments) to adapt themselves to such new groupings of states as the establishment and maintenance of general peace may demand. Thus, if one European union or a group of European unions is to be associated in some form of general organization with the Pan American community, it may well be necessary to bracket Canada with the latter. This should not disrupt a Commonwealth flexible enough to accommodate, among other curiosities, such a constitutional rarity as Eire.

In France more was heard about destroying the strength of Germany than about the possibility of winning her, under a new regime, into federalized co-operation for the peace and welfare of Europe. Nevertheless, French voices were not lacking in the federalist refrain. Speaking in the Senate on December 30, 1939, Premier Daladier foreshadowed a federal association of the states of Europe, and an active group of parliamentarians held discussions on the same theme. *Les Nouveaux Cahiers* contained a series of studies on federalism; Jacques Maritain published a long article entitled "Europe and the Federal Idea" in *The Commonweal* for April 19 and 26, 1940, and the same thought is to be found in Denis Saurat's contribution, "French Aims," to *The Fortnightly* for April 1940.

Among the French literature on the subject, one article merits special attention. It is by Georges Scelle, professor in the University of Paris, author of highly esteemed books on international law, and appears under the title "Le Problème du Fédéralisme" in *Politique Etrangère* for April 1940.

Professor Scelle points out that, whereas the English reject permanent repression as a solution of the problem of aggression and pin their hopes to the possibility of co-operation with a regenerate Germany, the French on the other hand have been driven by repeated bitter experience to the conviction that only force will serve. Even in France, however, there is a minority which takes the English view, and Professor Scelle sees a bridge between the two attitudes in the suggestion that there should be a considerable period between an armistice which would exact conditions of immediate security and the final peace settlement which would draw the forms of permanent European government. Feelings, as well as conditions, might change during this interval.

Professor Scelle himself regards gradual federation as the method of political progress dictated by the inescapable trend toward larger organized communities—a trend which is itself the response to that closer integration of human society brought about by scientific and industrial development.

Like so many recent writers, to say nothing of political

orators, he starts from the Anglo-French union for war purposes. In peacetime the Supreme Council would be subordinated to an interparliamentary body composed of national delegations whose membership would be drawn from the different parliamentary parties and groups in proportion to their strength. This would constitute, though at second hand, representation of all important popular interests and shades of opinion. Voting in this body would be by individuals, not by national delegations, and Professor Scelle would have its decisions immediately valid, though he thinks that a rule of national ratification might work in the period of interallied good will which might last for some time after victory.

An intergovernmental body, corresponding to the Supreme Council existing when Professor Scelle wrote, would initiate, co-ordinate and execute decisions of the quasi-parliament, operating through a common secretariat.

To this nucleus other states would adhere, beginning with Belgium, Holland and Switzerland, which are those most closely related geographically and ideologically to Britain and France. This Western Federation would require no second chamber representing the states, a problem made difficult by the vast disparity in strength and the confusion between legal and substantial, or "functional," equality. Professor Scelle points out that these chambers designed to safeguard state interests have in fact always abandoned that character and become, like the second chamber in unitary states, merely a part of the machinery serving the interest of the collectivity as a whole.

Not wishing to embarrass his nascent federation with a multiplicity of institutions, Professor Scelle is content with the existing Permanent Court of International Justice as an agency for the settlement of disputes as to facts and rights. Claims calling for a modification of present rights (touching, that is to say, on the familiar problem of peaceful change) could only be finally disposed of by reference to the highest political organ of the federation.

Germany is not admitted into this Western Federation.

Federation assumes a certain homogeneity of political doctrine. It can exist between republics and constitutional monarchies, but not, our author declares, between dictatorships and democracies. The best that he can do with Germany for the near future is to allow her to organize herself as a federation, one of a whole series of federations, parallel to that of the West and including one for the Scandinavian, one for the Baltic, one for the Balkan, and perhaps even one (interlapping with some of the preceding) for the Mediterranean countries.

Russia is Asiatic, destined to form a federalized world by herself. She and Germany must be isolated from one another by strong European federal groupings. This opinion appears again in R. L. Buell's *Isolated America.*

As an organ of co-operation between these numerous federations, and between them and other regional groupings such as the Pan American Union, Scelle would re-establish the League of Nations, this time with the official collaboration of the United States. The League would be a sort of federation of federations, not interfering in the internal government of its member federations, but co-ordinating measures for the administration of interests which transcend regional boundaries and become universal. Scelle specifies as examples interests of an economic, cultural and philanthropic character. In these fields, as in others, there exist universal needs and aspirations which must be defined and satisfied.

Students of the spontaneous manifestations of the *Zeitgeist* may be interested to follow the federal idea about the world. The following papers are worth mentioning as a few more mileposts along the way: for Switzerland, the article by Professor William Rappard in *L'Esprit International* for January 1940; for Germany, Hans Schmidt's "Germany— The Voice from Within" in *Harper's* for June 1940; for Australia, F. W. Eggleston's "Long-Term Aims of the War" in the *Austral-Asiatic Bulletin* for December-January 1939- 1940. The United States has not been less prolific than England. Alfred M. Bingham's *The United States of Europe* and Raymond L. Buell's *Isolated America,* both much wider in scope than their titles would suggest, accept the federal principle as the way to peace in Europe and set their projects for union in that continent against a background of universal economic and political organization. Among the many shorter contributions to the same theme, I shall mention only Grenville Clark's *Memorandum on a Federation of Free Peoples,* Felix Morley's article "The Formula of Federation," in *Asia,* June 1940, and the cogent brief for a group of regional federations in which the United States would play an active part, published by James P. Warburg under the query, *Peace in Our Time?*

Whether all of this thought and writing is destined to shape the future of international politics, or to join the designs of St. Pierre, Crucé and Sully in the museum of utopian dreams, its volume and its geographical distribution make it a characteristic of the mind of our time, and as such it deserves to be recorded and interpreted. In no age has there been so widespread a conviction that war is a tragic folly which can be avoided by a rational organization of the community of mankind. Those who observe the manifestations of this conviction may find in them compelling evidence of the upward progress of the human spirit.

CHAPTER V

THE INTER-AMERICAN SYSTEM

Relatively little attention has been paid in studies of world organization, actual or prospective, to that society of American Republics which holds periodical Pan American Conferences and maintains, as a permanent secretariat and agency of documentation and information, the Pan American Union at Washington. The decline in the influence of the League of Nations, which set in with the Manchurian failure of 1932, the rapid approach to war in Europe, and finally the outbreak of hostilities in 1939, have all tended to knit together the loose organization of the Western hemisphere and to make of it a serviceable instrument for the defense of territorial, political and economic interests against threatened aggression. As other peace-structures crumble, the American nations seek support for their own security and well-being in the association which, after a number of false starts dating from the early nineteenth century, has since 1889 been steadily extending the material range of its activities and acquiring cohesive strength.

Students of politics looking at the Pan American practice of conference and consultation are baffled by the vagueness of what, for want of a better name, we may call the articles of association governing this collaboration. Until 1928 there was nothing but a series of resolutions adopted by successive conferences to serve as a fundamental act binding these nations together and defining the functions of their fellowship. Before that date no treaty had been drafted to establish a general framework for their joint activities. The term "Pan American Union," popularly used to express the idea of a community of American states meeting in periodic conference and engaging in joint enterprises that range from measures of public health to the codification of international law, officially applies only to the office at Washington. This was first established at the conference of 1889 by resolution, and the same form of decision was employed by subsequent conferences to amend its construction and extend its duties.

At the sixth conference, held at Havana in 1928, a longstanding desire to give the Union a fixed constitution not to be changed by mere resolution bore fruit in a formal draft convention. This convention is to come into force only on ratification by all twenty-one republics, which has not yet happened. The text is however little more than declaratory of existing purpose and practice, and an analysis will therefore reveal the nature of the association as it now is.

If and when ratified, the Havana Convention of 1928 will give the solemn authority of international treaty to the name "Union of American States" in a sense which includes the whole mechanism of collaboration. The Santiago Conference had in 1923 resolved "To confirm the existence of the Union of the Republics of the American Continent, which maintains under the name of the 'Pan American Union' the institution which serves as its permanent organ." But the Havana Convention puts the same decision into a form which requires ratification on behalf of the consenting states and which on ratification would become a legally binding international agreement. No modification would then be possible except by amendment similarly adopted and ratified.

The preamble declares the purpose of this union of the American states to promote "the harmonious development of their economic interests and the co-ordination of their social and intellectual activities" and recognizes the place of law in the regulation of intercourse between peoples.

Article I gives a treaty basis not only to the Pan American Union but to the conferences as well. The text is as follows:

The Union of the American States tends to the fulfilment of its object through the following organs:
  (a) The International Conference of American States.

(b) The Pan American Union under the direction of a Governing Board, with its seat in the city of Washington.

(c) Every organ that may be established by virtue of conventions between the American States.

Each State enjoys as of right representation at the Conferences and on the Governing Board.

Article XII specifically recognizes the right of each contracting state to withdraw from the Pan American Union at any time. But such withdrawal would probably not mean withdrawal from the Union of the American States, which is described in the preamble as a moral union resting "on the juridical equality of the Republics of the Continent and in the mutual respect of the rights inherent in their complete independence," and which is apparently regarded as something having an independent existence merely confirmed by such instruments as the Santiago resolution of 1923 already cited.

The Havana Convention of 1928, which, if it is ever ratified by all the American republics, will be the nearest thing to a constitutive covenant of the Union of American States or Republics (the words seem to be used indifferently), contains no mutual guarantees of territory, no promises of military or financial assistance in the event of aggression, no stipulations for sanctions against an aggressor, no obligation to submit disputes to peaceful settlement, and no undertaking to disarm. All such matters have been left to be dealt with in separate agreements if at all. Unlike the League of Nations, which was built up all in one piece and whose members assumed immediate obligations under each of the above heads, the Union of American States has been only a moral or ideal entity. When its existence and character were expressed in a formal act intended to become legally binding on ratification, the members undertook nothing more than to "continue their joint action of co-operation and solidarity by means of periodic meetings of the International Conferences of the American States, as well as by means of organs established by international agreements, and through the Pan American Union . . ."

Even this vague and general undertaking is qualified by the explicit right of immediate withdrawal from the Pan American Union on payment of the current year's contribution.

The Union of American States (and the full title must be used to distinguish the general organization from its specific organ, the Pan American Union) has not rested on this statement of intention to co-operate. It has, as the need was felt and occasion presented itself, proceeded to implement its ideal community with working institutions. We propose now to sketch its machinery and achievements.

(1) The Constitution and Work of the Pan American Union

Founded by resolution of the first in the modern series of Pan American Conferences, that held at Washington in 1889, the "Commercial Bureau of the American Republics" was charged with the compilation and distribution of commercial information. Subsequent conferences made specific provision for its direction and added to its duties, that of Buenos Aires in 1910 changing its name to "Pan American Union." It is directed by a Governing Board consisting of representatives of all the American republics, who annually elect their own Chairman, and who appoint the Director General and Assistant Director. Other personnel is appointed by the Director General with the approval of the Board, the positions being distributed as far as possible among the nationals of the members of the Union. At its regular meeting in November the Board passes the budget and determines, in proportion to population, the share to be paid by each member. The Pan American Union is situated permanently at Washington, in a building constructed from a fund established as to three-quarters by Andrew Carnegie and as to one-quarter by contribution from the various republics.

The Union serves as a permanent Commission for the International Conferences of American States, keeping their records, preparing their agenda, and drafting regulations for their proceedings. It compiles, circulates and preserves information covering all the treaty relations of the American states, their tariffs, labor legislation, resources, industries, their systems of public instruction and public health. It publishes a monthly bulletin carrying articles on any matter within its wide range of interests. Political activities are expressly forbidden it by a resolution adopted at Havana in 1928, as well as by the Convention drawn up at the same Conference. The Governing Board is subject to the same rather vague prohibition, which is probably intended to avert any tendency toward functions such as those performed by the Council of the League of Nations. This caveat has not prevented increasing use of the Pan American Union as a center and co-ordinating agency of the ever expanding activities of this Western community of nations.

(2) The International Conferences of American States

Simon Bolivar called the first Pan American Conference at Panama in 1826, and attempted there to establish a confederation of the revolted colonies of Spain. The United States was invited, but owing to prolonged debate on the appointment of representatives in Congress the survivor of the two delegates finally sent never got to the meeting. At intervals during the next fifty years varying groups of the Spanish-American republics met in conferences usually aimed at continental union. This principal object was of course never achieved, but some subsidiary progress was made in the regulation of commerce and the protection of trade marks and copyright. It was only in 1889 that the first full assembly of the American republics took place. The Conference which met in that year at Washington on the initiative and under the chairmanship of James Blaine, Secretary of State, and which took the important step of creating, in the Commercial Bureau of the American Republics, at once a visible symbol and an active instrument of the sense of community among the nations of the hemisphere, was officially the beginning of the current development in Pan Americanism. Three similar meetings had taken place at irregular intervals up to 1923. The fifth Conference met that year at Santiago de Chile, and there has been a regular Conference every five years since. Five years were fixed as the maximum interval in the draft Havana Convention of 1928. In addition, there have been numerous Commercial, Sanitary and Scientific Congresses, as well as the Washington Conference on Conciliation and Arbitration, 1929, and the Inter-American Conference for the Maintenance of Peace held at Buenos Aires in December 1936.

A Convention drawn up at Buenos Aires in 1936 made provision for consultation among the American governments in the event of any threat to their peace. Two years later the Declaration of Lima specified that this consultation should take the form of meetings of the Ministers for Foreign Affairs at the summons of any one of them. These meetings, two of which have been held since the outbreak of war in Europe, are to be clearly distinguished from the International Conferences of American States. They are a less elaborate method of joint deliberation, designed to meet emergency conditions; and the record of the first two, held at Panama and Havana respectively, indicates that they may be notably effective in the co-ordination of political and economic defense.

The deliberations of the Conferences have ranged over the whole field of interests common to the American nations. A large proportion of their resolutions are little more than high-sounding reiterations of hemispheric solidarity, declarations of alleged common conceptions of democracy, liberty and autonomy, and promises of vague collaboration. Many of their formal conventions have failed of ratification and so have never come into operation. Somehow, nevertheless, they have established institutions and brought to bear influences which have modified national policies and softened the clash of conflicting interests. They have not prevented all war in the hemisphere; but practices of mediation have helped to shorten hostilities, and the habit of frequent discussion, anticipating and neutralizing causes of conflict, impedes the growth of those sharp rivalries which in the process of time might make war as endemic in America as it is in Europe. The development of sympathetic understanding is being accelerated by increased attention to cultural relations. Special conferences have been held in this field, and arrangements made for the exchange of teachers and students. The United States has shown the importance which it attaches to such means of enhancing the sense of community by creating a special division on cultural relations in the Department of State. The rest of this chapter is given to a summary of the products of Pan Americanism. It should not be forgotten that each has its roots in one or other of the Conferences.

(3) Commerce, Communications and Finance

Mention has already been made of the primary motive in establishing the Pan American Union, namely the compilation and communication of economic statistics. The second Conference, held at Mexico City in 1901, adopted a convention by which the states undertook to supply the necessary data to the Union, where it is classified and held available for reference. The monthly Bulletin, in English, Spanish, Portuguese and French, serves among other purposes as a vehicle for such information.

Besides this exchange of information on industry, agriculture, and commerce, successive conferences have been able to bring about a useful measure of uniformity in laws regarding patents, trade marks, bills of lading, port dues, consular fees and salvage. The Convention on Commercial Aviation drawn up at Havana in 1928 brings into operation among the American states a law of the air identical in its principles with that enacted in the Paris Convention of 1919, to which the United States and all but five of the Latin-American republics failed to become parties. The sovereignty of each state in its air space is recognized, but the parties to the Convention grant to their respective aircraft mutual right of passage subject to conditions of airworthiness for machines and competence for pilots.

Frequent movements have been initiated to reduce existing barriers to trade or at least to prevent the erection of new ones. These have resulted for the most part in nothing more substantial than resolutions proclaiming the firm adherence of the parties to the principle of unrestricted international commerce, while the "necessities" of the moment have prevented action on the principle. At the present, however, the loss of European markets owing to war and blockade has concentrated new attention on the problem of freeing the inter-American avenues of trade.

A Financial and Economic Advisory Committee has been set up following a resolution of the Meeting of Ministers of Foreign Affairs at Panama in 1939. This body, consisting of representatives of the twenty-one republics, is in permanent session at Washington, and it has been instructed by the Havana Meeting of Foreign Ministers to explore means of increasing the domestic consumption of, and inter-American trade in, commodity surpluses normally sent abroad. At the same time it is to devise machinery for storing and financing such surpluses pending their orderly marketing. A subsidiary body, the Inter-American Development Commission, is undertaking the task of increasing production in America of mineral, agricultural, forest and industrial products for which a new market can be found in this hemisphere now that the ordinary sources of supply have been stopped.

The Inter-American Financial and Economic Advisory Committee has drawn up and submitted to the governments for ratification a draft Convention establishing an Inter-American Bank. This institution is designed, to quote a portion of its draft by-laws:

(1) To facilitate the prudent investment of funds and stimulate the full productive use of capital and credit.
(2) To assist in stabilizing the currencies of American Republics.
(3) To function as a clearing house for, and in other ways facilitate, the transfer of international payments.
(4) To increase international trade, travel and exchange of services in the Western Hemisphere.
(5) To promote the development of industry, public utilities, min-

ing, agriculture, commerce and finance in the Western Hemisphere.

The authorized capital of the Bank is to be one hundred million United States dollars, divided into one thousand shares having a par value of one hundred thousand dollars each. Operations may be begun when at least five governments have ratified the Convention and subscribed to at least one hundred and forty-five shares of the stock.

Directly or through various sub-committees, the Inter-American Financial and Economic Advisory Committee is also laboring to improve shipping facilities, reduce freight rates and port dues, simplify and standardize customs procedure, and facilitate the movement of commercial travelers and samples. Much of this effort is a continuation of work begun years ago; but the effects of a war which has closed extra-American markets and sources of supply, and withdrawn foreign shipping services from American waters, are clearly apparent in the new vigor with which the multifarious problems of economic co-operation are being attacked. Clearly too the visible progress made by the Axis Powers in their campaign for commercial and political domination in Latin-America has awakened the United States to a sense of imminent danger, and the instinct of self-preservation now urges the leading American republic to throw her immense resources into the construction of a working economic community of the hemisphere. If she succeeds, the structure is likely to outlast the war now in progress and to play an important part in the international politics of the post-war world.

(4) Labor, Social Conditions, and Health

From the Conference of 1902 on, the Union of American States has taken a lively interest in questions of public health. Special conferences on the subject have been frequent, a Pan American Sanitary Bureau has been established, and a Pan American Sanitary Code has been elaborated. The directors of national public health services are brought together from time to time to share the results of their research and experience, and to discuss methods of training and organizing sanitary personnel. Several Conferences have been devoted to "Eugenics and Homoculture."

More recently similar attention has been turned to the improvement of the living and working conditions of labor. The fifth Conference, at Santiago in 1923, passed a comprehensive resolution preparing the way for collective study of legislation on collective bargaining and the relations between labor and capital, on the prevention of industrial diseases and accidents, and on unemployment, sickness and accident insurance. This was followed up by a resolution of the seventh Conference, at Montevideo in 1933, recommending the establishment of an Inter-American Labor Institute with headquarters in Buenos Aires. No action has been taken as yet upon this proposal, though the eighth Conference, at Lima in 1938, touched again on labor questions, specifically in the matter of migration and the working conditions of working women. Meanwhile the functions of such an institute are being exercised in fact by the International Labor Organization with its periodic special conferences in Latin America.

(5) *International Law and Adjudication*

Practically all the Pan American Conferences have abounded in resolutions favoring obligatory arbitration of international disputes, and the various republics were party to more than a hundred treaties embodying this principle. The Gondra Treaty, drawn up at Santiago de Chile in 1923, was designed to establish a system of investigation and report for all disputes between members of the Union. It was revised at Washington in January 1929, and made part of a plan of peaceful settlement by conciliation or arbitration. This plan has now come into operation, the relevant Conventions having been ratified by eighteen of the American states.

The Washington Conference, which met specially for this purpose, produced two Conventions, one on arbitration, the other on conciliation. In the first, the parties bind themselves to submit to arbitration disputes of a legal nature, disputes, that is to say, which can be settled by the application of legal principles. The only exceptions are disputes that fall within the domestic jurisdiction of the parties or concern a state not bound by the Convention. When an actual case presents itself, the parties may either make their own agreement as to the composition of the arbitral tribunal or have recourse to the arrangements for that purpose embodied in the Hague Convention of 1907.

In the Conciliation Convention, the obligation of submission is not limited to disputes of a legal nature. The Gondra Treaty had constituted permanent commissions at Washington and Montevideo, consisting of the three longest-accredited American diplomatic representatives in each of these capitals, through which any party to a dispute might address to the other a request for the appointment of a board of inquiry. But neither they, nor the boards of inquiry, were authorized to arrange a settlement. What was intended was strictly inquiry and report. The Washington Convention of 1929 uses these permanent commissions for the same purpose in the initiation of proceedings, but gives them in addition authority to act in a conciliatory capacity pending the appointment of a special conciliation commission. On the demand of a disputant, indeed, they must so act. The conciliation commissions are composed of five persons, two (of whom one only may be a national) appointed by each of the parties in dispute and one (who acts as president) selected by these four. From the beginning their object is to bring about a settlement, but if they do not succeed in doing so while in session, they in any case investigate the cause of difference and draw up a report by majority vote. This has not the force of an arbitral award; but the parties are bound not to seek a settlement by other than amicable means for six months after the report is communicated to them. The conciliation proceedings may be broken off at any time by a settlement, or by an agreement to refer to arbitration or to adjudication by a court of international justice.

In 1908 the five Central American states established a Court of Justice with jurisdiction over all disputes between them that failed of diplomatic settlement. In the ten years of its existence the Central American Court of Justice gave judgment in eight cases, but two of its decisions aroused political opposition which prevented the renewal of the Treaty of Washington on which it was based. Legally, this tribunal enjoyed a considerable reputation, and the circumstances of its discontinuance have not discouraged the movement in Pan American circles to establish an Inter-American Court with jurisdiction extending to all the republics of the hemisphere. Several proposals to this end have been brought before the Conferences, but action upon them was again postponed at Lima in 1938.

On top of all these arrangements for peaceful settlement comes the Argentine Anti-War Pact, concluded at Rio de Janeiro in 1933 and ratified by some European states as well as by twenty of the American republics. This is another condemnation of aggressive war; but it adds to the principles of the Pact of Paris an explicit undertaking not to recognize territorial acquisitions made by force of arms, and a positive obligation to submit disputes to conciliation. A detailed procedure of conciliation is laid down for disputes between states not already bound by similar agreements.

A frequent item on the Pan American agenda is the codification of international law. At Mexico City in 1902 and at Rio de Janeiro in 1906 agreements were approved calling for the establishment of a jurists' committee to prepare a code for submission to the governments. The agreement of 1906 resulted in the Commission of American Jurists, which held its first meeting in Rio de Janeiro in 1912. This body met again in Rio in 1927 and examined a series of draft conventions prepared on the invitation of the Governing Board of the Pan American Union by the American Institute of International Law, an unofficial organization comprising representatives of the different societies of international law in the American republics. Twelve drafts were passed on to the Havana Conference of 1928, where eight were adopted and opened for ratification by the states. These had to do with the status of aliens, treaties, diplomatic agents and consuls, rights of neutrals in sea warfare, asylum for political refugees, and the duties of states in civil war.

The same Conference adopted the Bustamante Code of Private International Law, which has since been ratified by fifteen of the American republics and is in force in their territories. This is a considerable accomplishment, for it means the adoption of uniform rules for the solution of what is often called the conflict of laws. The commencement of transactions in one country and their completion in another, the birth or marriage of persons in one country and their residence in another, the succession to property owned in one state by the nationals of another, are all matters in which one of several national laws may be applied, and it is the business of private international law to say which shall determine the questions at issue.

Nationality, extradition, and the rights and duties of states were the subject of further conventions adopted at the seventh Pan American Conference, Montevideo, 1933. In an attempt to expedite the slow process of codification, a Committee of Experts was at the same time set up to assist in the preparation of drafts. This forms part of what now, after further revision by the Lima Conference in 1938, constitutes an unnecessarily complicated network of national and international agencies all working for the progressive codification of international law. Each of the republics is asked to establish a National Committee. These transmit their studies to Permanent Committees at Rio, Montevideo, and Havana, which in turn pass their work on to the Committee of Experts. The Experts prepare drafts and send them through the Pan American Union to the Commission of American Jurists now known as the International Conference of American Jurists. This Conference, which meets on summons by the Pan American Union, may reject, amend or adopt the drafts, which, after it has passed on them affirmatively, are in final form for ratification by the states.

In addition to this permanent machinery of codification, the Meeting of Ministers of Foreign Affairs of the American Republics in 1939 established a special committee to deal with urgent problems connected with the common neutrality of these republics in the war now waging in Europe. The Inter-American Neutrality Committee, consisting of seven members, has prepared and recommended to the governments a detailed system of rules in regard to internment, vessels used as auxiliary transports of warships, the entry of submarines into American waters, the inviolability of postal correspondence, and restrictions on the use by belligerents of telecommunications in neutral waters or territory.

(6) Political Co-operation

When the United States delegation proposed that a Permanent Inter-American Consultative Committee should be instituted by the Buenos Aires Conference in 1936, the Argentine Foreign Minister, Dr. Saavedra Lamas, opposed the suggestion on the ground that anything resembling a political organization of the American states would be out of harmony with the tradition of the Conferences. Certainly the delegation of authority to any joint body to impose any course of action upon the states has been carefully avoided, witness the repeated proviso that the Pan American Union shall not undertake any political activity. The Union and the Conferences propose; the states retain the liberty to comply or not. Resolutions, recommendations, and declarations form the bulk of the proceedings, and when the difficult operation of adopting a convention is completed the text must still be ratified by the states to become binding. This rejection of commitment in advance explains why so many painfully elaborated agreements have remained an empty record of declared intention without practical sequel.

Progress has gone somewhat further in regard to the pacific settlement of disputes. The states have bound themselves to submit to arbitration or conciliation. Submission to arbitration here as elsewhere carries with it the obligation to act in accordance with the award. No such obligation is implied in the conciliation process; but the commissions have been given power to initiate this process of their own motion, and the states have bound themselves not to embark on hostilities pending a report and for six months thereafter.

These are measures of a political nature even in a narrow conception of that ill-defined category. There is more than this, however. Particularly since 1936, when the Inter-American Conference for the Maintenance of Peace was held in Buenos Aires, the Pan American organization has been brought into service for the achievement of immediate and vital aims in international politics. Through its declarations of a common front against the threat of aggression from without, empty as these are of legal sanction, it is being used to warn off intervention and invasion. Of the Monroe Doctrine, previously resented as the imposed decision of one Great Power, it has made a joint statement of collective purpose. Its resolutions of common neutrality and the joint measures taken to ensure uniform neutral practice are matters of high policy. The plan adopted at Havana in July 1940 for the administration of European possessions in the Western Atlantic in the event of attempted changes of sovereignty, is as truly political as the mandate system under the League of Nations. By an artificial distinction we may classify as nonpolitical the steps taken at Panama and Havana to alleviate the economic effects of the war; but we cannot do as much for the effort to promote co-ordinated action against fifth-column conspiracies. Everything done by the Meetings of Ministers of Foreign Affairs is still *ad referendum*; but the very practice of holding such meetings and taking counsel together is as clearly political method as the holding of a federal parliament or league assembly. The fact that the results may not have the same immediate legal quality is not sufficient reason for placing them in a totally different category of activity.

Some importance attaches to understanding the Inter-American System for what it is. At the most recent Conferences there has been pressure from certain Latin-American countries for development in the direction of a League of the Western Hemisphere, complete with courts and sanctions. Consideration of these projects has been postponed by reference to the International Conference of American Jurists, which is to submit recommendations regarding them to the ninth Pan American Conference at Bogota in 1943. It is extremely doubtful whether these desires for greater certainty, for a more firmly implemented community, can overcome surviving prejudice against alliances and leagues. Such doubt should not blind us to the fact that, while in outward form preserving for its members the precious fetish of "their juridical equality as sovereign states," the Pan American organization is in actual practice, and as the need presents itself, assuming some of the functions of a hemisphere legislature and government. The process is the historically familiar one by which many enduring political institutions have evolved without preliminary constitutional enactment.

Some observers, comparing the laborious but steady growth of this association with the swift rise and fall of the League of Nations, are inclined to infer a general superiority in this mode of slow development and to adopt it as the only sound pattern of international organization. Why cannot Europe do as we have done?

The answer is manifold. Boundary disputes have embittered relations and sometimes led to war between American states. But the abundance of space in ratio to population has prevented these conflicts from assuming the intensity of European quarrels over territory. The pressure of population in one area has found a ready outlet in new lands close at hand. There has never been the same complexity or rivalry of races each with its convenient conviction of world mission. No balance-of-power tradition has taken root with its swift succession of competing and shifting alliances. The vast dominance of the United States, not always altruistic, sometimes grasping, but of recent years exercised steadily in the interests of peace and order, contrasts strongly with the endemic struggles of the Great Powers of Europe to gain and hold hegemony. An initial sense of community, born of the common battle for liberty from European control, has never quite lost its rallying force.

The generous endowment of territory, resources and opportunity, racial homogeneity, the shared struggle for establishment, and the presence of a single regulatory Power, have combined to create an environment more favorable to political co-operation and cohesion than has ever existed in Europe. The real force of that cohesion is still unknown, and those who boast of the Pan American method are shouting before the trial of strength. But even if the inchoate hemisphere community stands united against the growing threat of Germany and her allies, its survival will not prove it to be the model for regional organization elsewhere. The elements of its success will still be American, not to be found in Europe or in the Far East. There the problems are too aggravated and too immediate to allow of such leisurely solution as has been worked out for those of the Western hemisphere. There a planned settlement, capable of evolution certainly but ready for immediate application in its essential outline, a settlement compressing into a few months progress which has taken decades here, will be required to clear the ground and secure the framework for orderly development. The adoption of a single and universal method to meet radically different needs is one demonstrated defect of the League set up in 1919.

CHAPTER VI

PEACE IN THE PACIFIC

Current studies of organization for the prevention of war and the advancement of economic and social progress concentrate largely on Europe. There is a tendency to assume that if the frequent conflicts of that continent can be settled without violence, peace in the rest of the world will follow as a matter of course. It can be conceded that Europe is the center of the problem, and there is therefore considerable justification for making it the first and principal subject of international planning. But the peoples of Europe have vast interests in the Far East, and out of their competition in that area may arise direct conflict at home.

Colonial possessions are a case in point. Some of the most prized of these lie in the Pacific, and the equitable distribution and administration of colonial interests—a question with which every European plan must eventually deal—may depend quite as much upon developments in the Far East itself as upon any arrangements made between European Powers.

Stability of international relations in the Pacific, again, is a condition precedent of disarmament—a fact clearly recognized in the Washington Treaties of 1921. Disarmament in turn is conceded to be a condition of peace everywhere. The failure of the League of Nations (and of the Nine Power and Four Power Pacts) to settle the dispute between Japan and China over Manchuria was the beginning of the League's rapid decline, the weakness thus displayed in the entire system of collective security, including the Briand-Kellogg Pact, being one of the reasons for the final demise of the struggling Disarmament Conference.

Political considerations of this order are in themselves sufficient grounds for the belief that the reorganization of Europe cannot be more than a beginning, though a necessary beginning, of the structure of world order. They are reinforced by economic considerations. If international trade and investment, and the expanding welfare which they bring, are necessary to peace, then international economic planning must cover the Orient with its markets, its essential raw materials, its opportunities for development and the scope they offer for the industries and the finance of the West.

Of late years there has been a notable growth of scientific studies devoted to the political, economic and social problems of Far Eastern countries. Some of these have worked out in considerable detail the conditions of an equitable and enduring settlement of the long struggle between Japan and China. Few have attempted to plan the structure of any permanent order for the Pacific. Those that have done so seem content to advocate the renewal and reinforcement of the Nine Power Treaty. They would bring in the Soviet Union, they would establish a court for the disposal of regional disputes, and they would have an agreement for vigorous action against any violator of the treaty.

These recommendations count upon active, controlling and prolonged participation of the United States, Great Britain, and a few other Western countries in the politics of the Far East. The principal object is to remove any justification for present or future aggression on the part of Japan, and to stop such aggression if it occurs after equitable satisfaction of any genuine grievances has been offered. This is undoubtedly the central and immediate problem of peace in the Pacific. But the means of solving it in any permanent fashion may lie in developing defensive and progressive forces in the area itself rather than relying on intervention from outside.

Emphasis on China and Japan, and on external initiative, is prominent in the proceedings of the Virginia Beach meeting of the Institute of Pacific Relations, November-December, 1939. *Problems of the Pacific, 1939,* which is a record of the discussion, reports that "most members of the Study Meeting were agreed as to the objectives which any

Far Eastern settlement should endeavor to attain. Briefly, they may be summarized as the establishment of Chinese independence, a permanent change in Japan's policy toward China, and effective provision for Western aid and participation in the development of a stable and progressive economy in both China and Japan." Chinese independence means, according to an earlier passage in the report, that "China must be free from any form of foreign control, either political or economic," and this involves, among other important developments, "the abolition of all special privileges now enjoyed by foreign Powers under the system of unequal treaties." Extraterritoriality must go, concessions and settlements must be returned to China, troops and ships of war must be withdrawn.[1]

The same principles will be found reaffirmed and documented in the trenchant study by Nathaniel Peffer, published by the Institute of Pacific Relations under the title *Prerequisites to Peace in the Far East*. Professor Peffer, however, adds another condition, namely that the Western Powers begin gradually to relax their control over all their Eastern dependencies and encourage the rise of these communities to the full stature of nationhood.

It is this last condition that opens up the longest vista of internal progress together with the prospect, however distant and difficult of approach, of regional self-reliance. But how is the withdrawal of foreign control, and of the measure of protection that goes with control, to be accomplished without creating a vacuum into which Japan, or conceivably a victorious and strengthened China, would be free to thrust an Eastern imperialism which might prove far more nefarious than that of the West?

This is one of the problems to which Mr. W. L. Holland addresses himself in a memorandum prepared for the Institute of Pacific Relations on *The Far East in a New World Order*. The dependencies of Western states in the Far East lie principally in Southeast Asia, ringed about the South

---

[1] Kate L. Mitchell and W. L. Holland, *Problems of the Pacific, 1939*, New York, 1940, pp. 112 and 129.

China Sea. The growth of nationalism in this area, particularly in the Netherlands Indies, the Philippines, Burma and Indo-China, is in itself sufficient to make the interests of these countries an unavoidable part of the whole problem of peace in the Orient and the world. It is a new and gathering force which cannot be indefinitely suppressed, and it will achieve increasing autonomy for the indigenous peoples.[2] That autonomy is likely to find expression in perpetual strife, as it has in Europe, unless it is led into channels of constructive co-operation by wise direction in the near future.

The great question, that must be answered by anyone envisaging an organization that would utilize all available indigenous energies for the maintenance of order in Eastern Asia, is how to provide an effective counterweight to the present overwhelming power of Japan or the possible future power of China. In Mr. Holland's opinion, a close association of the Netherlands Indies, the Philippines, Burma and British Malaya would go some way to solving this problem, in addition to forwarding the special interests of these communities themselves. He therefore sets out a program of immediate action looking to this end.

At the present time the United States is co-operating informally with Great Britain, Australia and India to assist in the defense of Southeast Asia against the southward drive of Japan. Mr. Holland would substitute for this informal and *ad hoc* co-operation a treaty providing for the complete coordination of all needed measures of military and economic defense. The Netherlands East Indies, the Philippines, and Burma should appear at once as distinct parties to this treaty, though the participation of British Malaya would temporarily have to be through the government of Great Britain. Defense administration on the spot would be in the hands of a Regional Defense Board. There would be one commander-in-chief, and the treaty would provide for fixing from time to time the contributions of men, money and

[2] *Cf. Nationalism and Government in Southeast Asia*, by Virginia Thompson and Lennox Mills, Institute of Pacific Relations, in manuscript.

material to be required of the countries concerned. In this connection active measures should be taken for the training of indigenous troops, both officers and other ranks.

A technical advisory bureau should be organized immediately with headquarters at Singapore, Batavia or Manila, and branch offices elsewhere. Eventually this might be expanded to serve as secretariat for a general Far Eastern association; but its first function would be to study Indonesian problems, formulate policies and plan administrative machinery for regional co-operation. The way would thus be prepared for the establishment of a Joint Economic Council which would "co-ordinate the trade, industry, investment, public finance, migration and agricultural policies" of this group of countries. This co-ordination, which might ultimately lead to a customs and currency union with a central bank and investment board, would strengthen the group for military defense, protect it against a post-war slump, and prevent it from falling under the economic dictation of Japan or some other powerful trading nation.

Equal treatment in this Indonesian Union for the commercial and industrial enterprises of all peaceful nations would be guaranteed by treaty. No discriminatory tariffs, quotas or other restrictions would be permitted save as required in the clear interest of the indigenous population or as a sanction imposed on an offending state by a Far Eastern or universal association.

After the war Indo-China and perhaps also Thailand would be invited to join the Indonesian Union, and a program of public works and industrial development would be set on foot throughout the area. This would require outside capital, which the Joint Economic Council might borrow from the financial agency of a world-wide economic organization. The program of development would be accompanied by an intraregional exchange of technical experts and artisans, and by a carefully planned and supervised migration from overpopulated to underpopulated districts open for development.

This organization of the present dependencies encircling

the South China Sea would operate after the war in the setting of a wider Far Eastern association. Insofar as external aid continued to be needed for defense and administration, China, India and Japan would provide an increased proportion of personnel, subject always to proper safeguards for indigenous interests. Assuming loyal co-operation, they would enjoy full trading and investment opportunities in the territories of the Union. In particular, a co-operative Japan would have free access to the Indonesian markets for textiles and other light manufactures, and would receive in exchange the raw materials which she needs in quantity—iron ore from Malaya and the Philippines, bauxite from the Netherlands East Indies, coal from Indo-China, rice from Thailand, Indo-China and Burma.

Mr. Holland is far from making light of the difficulties involved in the formation of a Far Eastern security system; but he believes that this formidable task will be greatly lightened by the establishment of the Indonesian Union. "In terms of power," he observes, "the Far East will then consist of China, Japan, the U.S.S.R., India and the Indonesian Union. Within such a constellation an enduring equilibrium is at least conceivable. The Western nations would be in the picture but in a more stable and predictable fashion and their orderly withdrawal would be clearly provided for as the Asiatic nations achieved a working security system of their own."

The possibility of a regional security system in the Far East is not an essentially Western idea seeking to impose a schematic arrangement upon an alien and unwilling environment. For some years before 1937, when Japan resumed hostilities against China, there was talk of a Pact of the Pacific; and some of the warmest advocates of such a plan were Orientals.

Thus, among the data papers for the Banff Conference of the Institute of Pacific Relations in 1933 is one entitled *Some Considerations on the Future Reconstruction of Peace Machinery in the Pacific*. The authors are Professors Takaki and Yokota of the Tokyo Imperial University. One of the causes to which they attribute the failure of peaceable settlement in the Pacific is the absence there of a society of nations of similar development, and they recommend a regional organization with a treaty of security, nonaggression and arbitration.

The principal parties to this treaty would be China, Japan, the United States, the Soviet Union, Great Britain and France. It would be an amalgamation of the Nine and Four Power Treaties, the Briand-Kellogg Pact, and nonaggression treaties of the type initiated by the Soviet Union. The consultative procedure of the Four Power Treaty of 1922 is improved by the suggested use of conferences to examine disputes or threats of conflict and issue findings which, if concurred in by all members other than the disputants, would bind those members to act in accordance with their terms. The authors are anxious to avoid any sanctification of the *status quo*, and desire that their consultative process should be used as an instrument of peaceful change removing the causes of disputes before they develop. They therefore hope that the conference may meet periodically. Their treaty would prohibit recognition of any situation brought about by force, and would require the submission of all disputes, whatever their nature, to conciliation, arbitration or adjudication. Permanent conciliation commissions are to be set up between each pair of contracting parties for the settlement of any dispute not submitted to an arbitral tribunal or to the Permanent Court of International Justice.

Among Western writers who have adopted and developed these ideas, Raymond Leslie Buell devotes more than the usual perfunctory notice to the subject in his *Isolated America*. His recommendations regarding economic co-operation between Japan and China, the withdrawal of foreign military and naval forces from Chinese territory, cancellation of the unequal treaties, development programs and foreign loans, agree substantially with those already cited from *Problems of the Pacific, 1939*; but he goes much farther on the structural side. The parties to his re-enacted

Nine Power Treaty would agree on regular, not simply *ad hoc*, consultation; there would be a permanent Sino-Japanese conciliation commission, with alternative recourse to an arbitral tribunal or the Permanent Court of International Justice; and economic sanctions would be employed against treaty-violators. The reorganized League or Association of Nations, which Mr. Buell advocates as the necessary machinery of the general community of states, would have a special Pacific section of its secretariat, established perhaps at Manila, to carry on research in the social and economic problems of the area, to organize committees on fisheries, immigration, shipping and aviation, and to prepare the meetings of the Pacific Conference.

As for the colonies, Mr. Buell would have their possessors recognize the principle of trusteeship, which means the open door, the social and political advancement of native populations, and responsibility to an international colonial commission which would have the right of investigation on the spot.

Mr. Buell's study, like that of Professors Takaki and Yokota, provides ample evidence of the need for a special Pacific organization. Even though the world were ready for a powerful federation of all its states, the peculiar and complex problems of the Far Eastern area would require regional machinery decentralized and adapted to this particular environment. Remote control, without strong institutions constantly active on the spot, would be handicapped by distance and unfamiliarity.

No mere treaty, however definite its promise of joint action, can meet the case. The financial and economic assistance demanded for both China and Japan, the help and guidance needed for the economic and political development as well as the defense of the coveted dependencies, the sense of security and stability which alone induces labor for long-term objectives—all of these prerequisites of peace in the Pacific call for joint institutions of a legislative, administrative and judicial character in Eastern and Southeastern Asia.

In their early stages these institutions could not dispense with active participation from the United States, Great Britain, Holland and France. The orderly liquidation of their interests and responsibilities in the area, if nothing else, will demand the presence of these countries in the initial organization; and they will have to guarantee for an indefinite period security for the equitable interests of the indigenous peoples. But it should be made clear from the beginning that this Western guardianship is to be temporary only, and that its essential purpose is to develop sufficient strength, balance and cohesion in the Eastern League or Association to enable this to administer all regional business with the same measure of independence as that enjoyed by similar associations elsewhere.

Assuming the formation of an Indonesiân Union as a necessary element of equilibrium, the building of an effective Eastern League must still be a difficult and gradual process. No one imagines that it will spring full-fashioned from a single conference even if Japan is decisively defeated, or that it will evolve easily and swiftly under enlightened guidance and help from the United States, the Soviet Union and Great Britain. But the early determination and promulgation of a design to be worked to is surely in this instance, as in all long-term enterprises, a condition of ultimate success. The design itself will have to be agreed to by the prospective members of the association, and its elaboration is therefore a considerable undertaking which can hardly be begun too soon. The product of this preliminary operation should not be regarded as something to be adhered to slavishly, but as a tentative chart subject to alteration if and when important new factors present themselves.

In the Far Eastern grouping Mr. Holland would place China, Manchuria, Japan, the Indonesian Union, and India. The inclusion of Manchuria assumes that that territory will not be restored to China, though it may be under Sino-Japanese or international administration. The Soviet Union is not included, notwithstanding the proximity of its Pacific coast to Japan, and its long common frontier with China. It does not, in Mr. Holland's opinion, belong either culturally or economically to the group; and its interests in the area, like those of the United States and other countries bordering on the Pacific, are to be safeguarded by a wider Pacific organization. The latter is to include the United States, the U.S.S.R., Canada, Australia, New Zealand, the principal countries on the west coast of South America, and all the units of the specifically Far Eastern group.

It is a question worthy of discussion, however, whether this wider Pacific association will be necessary. As an alternative, I assume for the purposes of this chapter that something approaching a world commonwealth has been established, with membership and representation open to individual states. Problems involving all countries touching on the Pacific, as distinguished from those peculiar to Eastern Asia, can, it is suggested, be adequately handled by the World Commonwealth without the further complication of a distinct security system for the Pacific as a whole.

The Soviet Union, Australia and New Zealand would find their place in the World Commonwealth. Whether they should also form part of special regional groupings, European, Eastern, Pan American or other, is a question that may be left for decision as these associations develop. The essential nucleus of an Eastern League will be formed by China, Japan, India and the Indonesian Union. There is the focus of conflict in the Pacific, and there is the greatest need of joint institutions to preserve political security and facilitate economic progress. What follows is a tentative design for the organization of this Eastern League.

(1) China, Japan, India, and the Indonesian Union make a covenant of nonaggression, nonrecognition of the results of aggression, security, arbitration and economic and social co-operation.

(2) To carry out and enforce this covenant, they establish and maintain the following agencies as the essential institutions of an Eastern League:

(a) An Assembly, consisting of an equal number of delegates from each party, meeting regularly once a year and in special session as required, to act as legislative authority in matters of common interest, to direct and supervise the whole work of the Eastern League, to enact its budget, scrutinize its expenditure and provide for raising the necessary funds.

(b) A Military Commission, appointed by the Assembly, with the function of bringing about the reduction of national forces and equipment and, *pari passu,* the formation of a regional defense and police force.

(c) A Pacific Court, with compulsory jurisdiction in all disputes between the members of the Eastern League. Judges will be appointed by the Assembly on nomination by a Judicature Committee, which shall be one of the Assembly's standing committees and contain representatives of all the members.

(d) An Economic and Financial Commission for the joint administration of the special economic interests of the region. This Commission, like the two following, will work in close collaboration with the corresponding body of the World Commonwealth sketched elsewhere in this book,[3] and may constitute a regional branch of that body.

(e) A Commission on Social Legislation and Administration, to devise common measures of public health, labor regulation, migration, and control of injurious traffics. This may serve as regional branch or adviser of the bodies charged with these functions on behalf of the World Commonwealth.

(f) A Secretariat, with sections corresponding to the bodies listed above, for the clerical and research service of the whole organization.

The Assembly and Commissions must operate by majority. From the beginning the members should assume the obligation to join in economic, and as a last resort military, sanctions against a violator of the covenant. As rapidly as possible the Economic and Financial Commission and the Military Commission should be provided with the author-

[3] Chapters VIII, XI, XIII, XIV, XV and, for summary, Chapter XVII.

ity and means of executing sanctions without having to depend entirely on the concurrent action of the member states. In order to increase the objectivity and efficiency of these Commissions, they should include, in addition to representatives of the members, several experts not nationals of any community in the Eastern League.

To secure the dynamism demanded by all contemporary commentators on international organization, the Assembly should have the authority to change laws and legal situations imposing inequitable hardship. In this function, it might have the assistance of the Pacific Court, for before making changes it will be prudent to obtain an authoritative statement as to what the law is, and some advice on the direction which an amendment, if any, should take. This is particularly important in view of the ill-defined and controversial character of many portions of international law.

I have ventured to suggest a Pacific Court rather than a Conciliation Commission. Experience shows that the use of Conciliation Commissions is far from proportionate to the labor that has gone into their establishment. Their purpose is in large measure served by diplomacy. When that fails, the tendency is to submit a dispute, if it is presented for impartial settlement at all, to the more formal procedure of adjudication by a court or arbitral tribunal. Any difference between arbitration and adjudication has disappeared in modern practice.[4] It is believed, therefore, that a single tribunal can deal with all disputes between members of the Eastern League which can be disposed of by the application of law and equity.

[4] *Cf.* Chapter XIII on Supranational Courts.

CHAPTER VII

THE ORDER OF THE AXIS

One pertinent criticism of current plans for larger commonwealths after this war is that they complacently assume a complete victory by the democratic Powers. Frequently that assumption follows on the expressed conviction that supranational organization will be out of the question if the Axis wins. This ignores the sketches of a new order which are being thrown off from time to time in Germany, and, more vaguely, in Japan.

Before the military successes of 1940, there was already talk in Germany of *Grossraumwirtschaft*, a word which has since become something of a commonplace in discussions concerning Nazi policy. In its most generous connotation, the word seems to have meant a customs and currency union linking the states of continental Europe, exclusive of Russia, and having its center and controlling direction in Berlin. This was generous in that it presupposed more or less voluntary participation and, though certainly Germany was to be the senior partner, left a substantial measure of autonomy and some dignity to the other members of the partnership.

If, however, such a plan is to be credited to some of the leading economists and bankers of the Third Reich, it has lost its more liberal aspects in such official or semi-official statements as have appeared on the subject. The most explicit of these was that made by Dr. Funk, German Minister of Economics, on July 25, 1940.

Dr. Funk explicitly rejects customs and currency union. But he would organize Europe, always excluding Great Britain and the Soviet Union, as an economic unit dominated by Germany. Germany is to say what the surrounding satellite countries are to produce and what is to be done with the product. Manufacturing, particularly in the heavy and chemical industries, is to be concentrated in the expanded Reich, partly because of its relation to military power and partly because it produces more income than does agriculture. The industrialization which has been going on in eastern and southeastern Europe under sheltering tariffs is to stop, and the nations there are to devote themselves to improved farming.

The satellite states would keep their own currencies, holding them in stable ratio to the mark, which would be the international currency of Europe. Trading accounts between nations of the bloc would be expressed in marks and cleared through Berlin.

To the greatest possible extent, Germany would aim to make this European unit economically self-sufficient. There would inevitably, however, be deficiencies, and these would be supplied for the most part from Russia, China and the countries of South America. With these separate countries Germany would bargain, mainly in terms of barter, on behalf of the whole European unit, the control of this entire market enabling her to dictate advantageous conditions of exchange. Dr. Funk is quite explicit in his purpose of trading, outside Europe, with separate and independent states only. No dealings are to be had with any supranational trading bloc or cartel. The benefits of such organization are reserved for the Nazi regime in Europe.

The plan of satellite states, forming at once a buffer round Germany and a ring of jumping-off points if offensive war again becomes necessary, is said to be favorably regarded by the General Staff. But the General Staff, being concerned primarily with armed power and territorial security, and relatively indifferent to rates of employment and standards of living in Germany, would, it seems, treat the vassal nations with more kindness than Dr. Funk contemplates. Because agricultural improvements cannot be expected to increase production in proportion to the rapid growth of their population, the eastern and southeastern states at least are doomed by the Minister of Economics to increasing hunger and hardship. The Army, on the other hand, would like to keep them good-humored though dependent, prosperous though militarily paralyzed. It therefore deplores the dominance of German economic interest in the Funk project and for strategic reasons would inspire loyalty among the subject peoples by sharing with them the wealth of the Reich.

The same general pattern had already been adopted for Japan's "new order" in Eastern Asia. An empire supreme in military, naval and air strength rules its vast *Lebensraum* through puppet governments, exacts tribute of food and raw materials for its crowded population and busy factories, and sells its manufactures in a subject market closed to competitors. To the Western world, and now also to Australia, it sends the same invitation of mutual license as Nazi Germany has broadcast at each stage in its program of expansion—"Leave us alone in our back-yard and do what you like in yours." The newly appointed Japanese Minister to Australia, as reported by *The New York Times* of March 14, 1941, put the formula neatly—Australia for the Australians and Asia for the Japanese.

Neither the United States nor the British nations are quieted by this proffered segregation. For one thing, they have much reason to believe that the formula represents not an end but a method. Certainly it has served Germany as a means of securing undisturbed digestion of successive victims; and why should not Japan use a device so well proved? Moreover, British and American interests are too important in the region claimed by Japan, as in that claimed by Hitler, to be left to the tender mercies of totalitarianism. England and the Dominions (except Eire) have pledged their arms and all their resources to defeating the order of the Axis. The United States has promised and is furnishing them all aid short of direct belligerency for this purpose. In place of that order the democracies would set up a co-operating, democratic organization, which President Roosevelt, according to his message to Congress on January 6, 1941, would dedicate to establishing and maintaining, everywhere in the world, freedom of speech, freedom of religion, freedom from want, and freedom from fear.

President Roosevelt's ideal means, of course, democracy everywhere. As a goal toward which to work, that is admirable; but it cannot be reached immediately even by the utter defeat of the Axis. In the nearer future the democratic Powers, however triumphant, will be confronted with an urgent question suggested by the contrast between actual totalitarian doctrine and policy, on the one hand, and democratic aims on the other. Is democracy everywhere a condition precedent to real supranational order? This question assumes increasing importance with each new day of Russian resistance to the Nazi invasion. The mounting contribution of the Soviet Union to the ultimate defeat of Hitler will entitle it to a substantial voice in the organization of the post-war world, and there is little evidence to show that it will be ready to abandon dictatorship.

It should be clear, both from the doctrine of the masterrace and from the acts and declarations of the present regimes in Germany, Italy and Japan, that totalitarianism as they understand it implies the absolute discretion of the state in the external as in the internal sphere. Their doctrine predicates and their conduct expresses sovereignty in the full sense of the classical definition—power not subject to any human will other than that of its possessor. Only by a complete *volte-face* could they participate in any co-operative and representative organization. The core of such organization is a sense of community among the members and willingness to shape policy, at least to some degree, in conformity with the community interest as defined by joint authority.

But to say that no international organization could include Germany, Italy or Japan under their present regimes is not the same thing as saying that international organization is only possible between democratic states. That popular conclusion, if it is valid, must rest on other premises. We have not yet established a theoretical impossibility of associating democracies and dictatorships in one international or supranational community. A state without representative institutions, governed without responsibility to its people, might still place its relations with other states in the hands of an international authority constituted on representative lines.

Theoretically, international organization ought to be compatible with any form of government within the state which does not by its very nature violate the rights of other states or run counter to the interests of the organized international community.

Much depends upon the type of organization contemplated. The choice of organization will depend to some extent on the functions to be made common. Of the writers and statesmen who have discussed this question in relation to Europe, most are agreed that the establishment of centralized military forces must go along with national disarmament. This in itself practically implies federation, either in one union or in a series of regional European unions; and only the federal solution could make possible the important economic and social business which most projects assign to their central authority. Now union of the intimate federal type is scarcely conceivable if any of the members are to retain autocratic forms of administration. For one thing, the means by which such governments enforce obedience will be largely federalized. Also, if the federal authorities are to be elected at least in part by popular suffrage, the citizen would be enfranchised on the supranational plane though disenfranchised for national purposes. Finally, if the union were composed partly of dictatorships and partly of democracies, the political inequalities of the citizens would militate against stability. Projects of European union or unions therefore presuppose the spread of democracy.

At the other extreme, if we observe the working of an association as loose as the Pan American system (which in spite of its looseness is serving as a useful instrument in the slow development of an effective hemisphere community) we may be persuaded that dictatorships, whether *de facto* or *de jure*, may collaborate to some degree successfully in a so-called union of states. The same example tends to prove also that the functions of the organization are not quite conclusive in determining its form. Current developments may demonstrate that the Pan American Union can achieve economic and even defense co-ordinations which only federalization would make possible in Europe.

But is the type of international organization which can tolerate such differences in the form and methods of national government necessarily so weak as to be doomed to failure in any attempt to restrain a powerful state bent on realizing its own conception of its own interest? I doubt whether any simple answer of general validity can be given to this question. So long, for instance, as the United States continues to put its present quota of statesmanship (and money) into the Pan American system, that will probably serve to keep the peace and to make some social and economic progress in the Western hemisphere. The cynic will naturally remark that, under a façade of international democracy, this arrangement will amount to the same thing as the Nazi plans for Europe. Others will perceive a difference of substance as well as of form between the good-neighbor policy and the Funk plan.

We must not infer from the relative success of the inter-American system that a similar loose form of association will serve in Europe. It is at least doubtful whether the sharp conflicts of race, nationality and tradition in that continent can be reconciled by so casual an organization, even if it were directed by a state as powerful and as benevolent as the United States.

My general conclusion is that different types and different intimacies of association are likely to be needed in different parts of the world. Some of these may demand uniformity of political system, while others may endure disparity. If they are not to become merely larger units in a world struggle, they will need to be linked in some form of inchoate world community.

CHAPTER VIII

THE BRITISH-AMERICAN FRONT: COLLABORATION OR UNION?

As a democratic nation the United States has from the beginning of the war shown an unmistakable sympathy for Great Britain and her Allies. But until the downfall of France, the isolationism which had inspired the Neutrality Acts of 1935-1939 rejected the view that the American people were directly and materially concerned in the outcome of the struggle raging in Europe and Asia. From June 1940 on, the conviction grew that the ultimate design of the Axis Powers was world domination. With that conviction went the fear that the conquest of Britain would be followed not merely by a trade war with Germany which would be ruinous to manufacturers and producers in the United States, but possibly by direct threats to American territorial security. Almost overnight, defense became the most urgent national business, and, suddenly aware that England and her navy were America's first line of defense, a majority of the people rallied to the policy of "all aid short of war."

By successive steps—beginning with the acquisition of naval bases in the Western Atlantic colonies of Britain in exchange for fifty over age destroyers and carrying on through the Ogdensburg Agreement for a Permanent Joint Defense Board with Canada, the assignment of airplanes and other equipment to England, the "Lease-Lend" Act, the Hyde Park arrangement between President Roosevelt and the Prime Minister of Canada for further industrial and financial co-ordination in the production of material for continental defense and supplies to Britain—the United States has given concrete expression to the new realization of identity of essential interest with the fighting democracies.

By the spring of 1941, American naval patrols, operating a thousand miles and more out into the Atlantic, were assisting British warships in their work of convoy by information on the whereabouts of enemy raiders. Broadcasting on May 27, President Roosevelt said: "Our patrols are helping now to insure delivery of the needed supplies to Britain. All additional measures necessary to deliver the goods will be taken." Whether the aid now being given, or the further measures that may be adopted to prevent the conquest of England, shall result in active belligerency is clearly left to the choice of Hitler.

Nor does the identity of interest extend only to preventing an Axis victory. In the same speech the President not only said, "We will not accept a Hitler-dominated world." He added this: "And we will not accept a world, like the post-war world of the 1920's, in which the seeds of Hitlerism can again be planted and allowed to grow. We will accept only a world consecrated to freedom of speech and expression—freedom of every person to worship God in his own way—freedom from want—and freedom from terrorism."

Here, as in his message to Congress on January 6 in which he first specified "the four freedoms" as the foundations of the post-war world, the President of the United States pledges himself to the creation of a universal community more powerful and more progressive than the League of Nations. Within two days the British Foreign Secretary, speaking at the Mansion House in London, announced the British Government's acceptance of this program. "We have found," he said, "in President Roosevelt's message to Congress in January 1941, the keynote of our own purposes." And further—"as His Majesty's Government intend . . . to strive in co-operation with others to relieve the post-war world from want, so will they seek to ensure that the world is freed of fear."

To clear the way for the new age of political and economic security to which each has thus been dedicated, the United States and the British Commonwealth are, then, joined in the common enterprise of preventing the Axis

Powers from dominating the world. They are receiving incalculable assistance from China, whose epic defense has been an effective obstacle to Japanese expansion in the Southwestern Pacific, from the exile armies of countries that have been overrun in Europe, and now from the Soviet Union. But because they command so large a part of the military, industrial and economic resources of the anti-Axis world, the British and American peoples must provide both sinews of defense and striking power for victory. The undertaking is one of such magnitude that only the fullest and most perfectly co-ordinated mobilization of their material and spiritual strength will suffice for its accomplishment.

The struggle has already been long and violent enough to ruin vast quantities of industrial, commercial and domestic equipment. Factories, warehouses, office buildings, housing, docks, shipping have been destroyed, transport systems worn and damaged, to an extent which will require years of repair. The expansion of war industry, involving both the creation of new plant and the adaptation of existing installations to the manufacture of weapons and munitions, burdens the future with an immense problem of liquidation and refitting for peacetime requirements.

The elaborate and delicate mechanism of international trade and finance, already damaged by the economic war which preceded the outbreak of military hostilities, has been broken to fragments. Belligerent blockade, national controls over imports and exports, rationing of exchange, and the general subordination of all wants to the demand for supplies of war, have stopped the long-established channels of commodity interchange. Food is rationed in the warring and occupied countries, while it piles up in unprecedented stocks in the countries of production and the producers lack means to purchase other necessities. Every day of battle adds its quota of relief, readaptation and rebuilding to the unimaginable labor of post-war salvage.

Essential as the close partnership of the English-speaking peoples is for the winning of the war, it will be hardly less indispensable for the colossal reconstruction that the most complete military victory will leave to be done. Upon them will chiefly fall the task of keeping order while wrecked political communities are reshaped. But merely to provide the physical security for the rebuilding will be far from enough. Intelligent direction, and much of the material, will have to be provided. The United States, with the British nations, must be both architect and contractor. Here again active assistance may be expected from other peoples which have contrived to remain free, and from the governments in exile. But only the combined initiative and drive of the United States and British Commonwealth will galvanize the famished and broken victims of aggression into new constructive activity. Only their resources can furnish the wherewithal to build. Pacification, order, relief—these tasks will offer continued employment for all the agencies of co-operation set up for war purposes.

From the crushed and from the victorious peoples alike will rise the cry—"It must never happen again." Besides the immense job of immediate reconstruction, the British and American governments will have to assume, in response to universal and irresistible demand, responsibility for planning the long-term organization of peace. They must begin again the old attack on war itself.

How will they do this? Will they give permanent and constitutional form to the pooling of resources temporarily resorted to for success in war? For some time already an active movement has been on foot to persuade them to do just this. Mr. Clarence Streit and the "Union Now" organization are campaigning for the federal union of the United States and the nations of the British Commonwealth. This federation would be the nucleus of an organization designed to embrace ultimately the whole world. Other peoples, as they established independent and democratic governments, would be invited to adhere. The strength, security, prosperity and stability of the English-speaking union would make membership in it a coveted privilege and the goal of other nations.

It may be that the British peoples have suffered enough

by war to be willing to give up their cherished and somewhat haughty separateness. If the realization of the need of American aid has not yet completely eradicated a certain ineffable sense of superiority to all things American, it has at least driven it into a concealment maintained by all but the more irresponsible members of society. In any event this slight disdain, which is not unrequited, is hardly more profound than the asperity of some members of existing and successful federations toward one another.

There is little reason to believe, on the other hand, that the mass of citizens of the United States have so entirely abandoned their traditional distaste for entangling alliances as to accept close and permanent association with a group of states scattered all the way from the North Atlantic to the Southwestern Pacific. They have indeed moved sufficiently from their recent isolationism to supply Britain and the other nations resisting aggression with such tools of war as they can spare from their own defense requirements. They are moving into ever closer association with the British Commonwealth for the purposes of the war. This they are doing in their own interest, to strengthen what has come to be recognized as their first line of defense, and in response to an emergency. But from such temporary association to constitutional union is a very long way—a gap which could be closed only by a change in the American attitude much more spectacular than even the rapid transition from neutrality to "all aid short of war." Probably nothing but great suffering, and the conviction that there lay the only way of escape, could cause such a change; and the suffering has not yet crossed the Atlantic.[1]

Far from confirming any disposition to reunion with Britain, some esteemed observers of American opinion predict a powerful reaction into isolationism once the military phase of the conflict is over. This revulsion, they believe, will be no less strong if American aid develops into active belligerency involving expeditionary forces and, ultimately,

[1] The August 1941 survey of American opinion by *Fortune* shows only 6.9 per cent support for federation of the democracies.

an army of occupation in Europe. They argue that, as after the armistice of 1918, the people will think of little but the speediest possible return to a peace footing. The army itself, composed, as it will be, not of professional soldiers, but of citizens temporarily detached from their real occupations, will long for home as soon as the fighting is finished, and the taxpayer will demand immediate relief from the exactions and restrictions of a war economy. The voice of reason, urging the necessity of establishing peace on a permanent basis, will be lost in the clamor for demobilization.

This prophecy assumes that the people of the United States as a whole have learned no lesson from the sequel of the last war and the circumstances leading up to this one. Those who reject it say that it underestimates the growing American conviction that the peace and the living standards of the United States can be preserved only if the nation plays a part proportionate to its power in maintaining world peace. The whole possibility of effective supranational organization after this war depends on the accuracy of this second estimate of American tendencies. If isolationism once more triumphs, the other nations, even if they have the will, will not possess the means first to create order out of chaos and then to enforce it. The political and economic relations of states will revert to the pattern of the nineteen-thirties, a maze of temporary expedients with only one exit, war.

To discuss the forms of supranational association after the war is therefore to assume participation by the United States. Yet it would be folly to ignore the warning of reaction. There will be powerful manifestations, not only in the United States but in the British countries, of the very human hunger for relaxation after supreme effort. We must not count upon an indefinitely prolonged Anglo-American resolution to serve alone as world police. Our people may soon weary of the burden.

Prudence therefore suggests that as soon as it can safely be done, the responsibility for world order should be transferred to the broadest feasible association of states. The great question will be—How can such an association be most speedily and most solidly built?

Should we, even if the will were there, start from a federal union of the English-speaking nations, expecting that all good peoples, as they gain or regain competent democratic nationhood, will crave admission? Surely there is some question whether this beginning, assuming it possible, is the best approach to an undertaking whose success will depend in no small measure on psychological factors. Even though we should be quite clear in our own minds that the union from which we start is only the means to an end, and that the end is a universal federation of mankind in which the fullest practical effect will be given to the principle of equality, we could hardly expect the same confidence in those peoples who are at first outside the pale. Instead of inspiring the ambition to join our English-speaking group, might we not set up movements for the formation of counter-groups—movements which, weak and concealed at first, would strengthen as the horrors and privations of war receded into the past? In so powerful a federal nucleus, non-English-speaking peoples would be apt to see the prospect of permanent domination of whatever association might ultimately be achieved. "Anglo-Saxony" would loom over them in the guise of a perpetual leviathan with which no approach to substantial equality would ever be possible for any other member of the world federation. The fact that on admission they would presumably be given representation in the federal organs of government at least proportionate to their contribution of strength to the union would hardly overcome this misgiving. Oppositionist propaganda would find ready appeal to suspicions of a new Anglo-American imperialism.

Nor is it to be taken for granted that if Britain and the United States are ready for federation the rest of the world is remotely approaching that stage of cohesion. The need and the possibility of federation in various parts of Europe have been recognized by persons eminently qualified to speak for the nations concerned. Few of these, however, see any likelihood of a single union even for Europe, to say nothing of universal federation. Only as between a very limited number of peoples do the necessary sympathies and similarities exist.

It is freely admitted that the chief constructive forces in the period immediately following the cessation of hostilities must be American and British. From the English-speaking peoples, moreover, must come leadership in the supranational organization eventually adopted for the preservation of a lasting and progressive peace. But it may well be an illusion to pin our faith to an Anglo-American union in which the other nations would gradually merge. We shall probably have to make our new beginning with something much looser in the way of association than a federal union —an association in which other nations or groups of nations will share with British and American groups the status of original and constituent members. The surest path of progress may be to utilize existing associations, or tendencies to association, linking them together in one universal organization for purposes which transcend group boundaries, rather than to offer a single union to nations of widely different traditions, manners and political systems.

To sum up—for successful prosecution of the war, and to prevent its recurrence, the choice before the American and British peoples lies between 1) a federal union expanding as rapidly as possible into world federation; and 2) an alliance (whether formal or informal is of minor importance) used first to win the war and then to organize a universal association, similar in some respects to the League of Nations, supplementing and co-ordinating existing or potential associations in Europe, the Americas and the Far East.

The second of these arrangements, it may be conceded at once, has many imperfections. Its character, and the principal difficulties with which it will have to cope, form the subject of later chapters. In adopting it as the more practical method of preserving and enhancing our several ways of life I have been moved by two main considerations. One is that it has more prospect of general acceptance than federal union; the other, that it will run less risk of being torn apart by incompatibilities which are still too powerful to be safely compressed into a federal mold.

The joint declaration made by the President of the United States and the Prime Minister of Great Britain on August 14, 1941, far from hinting at federal union, avoids even such terms as alliance or association. The sole explicit reference to post-war organization as distinct from collaboration is contained in the paragraph which records the conviction that disarmament must be imposed first on potential aggressors, "pending the establishment of a wider and permanent system of general security." If there was any thought in the mind of either statesman of limited union as an intervening stage, no word of this pronouncement betrays it. In his speech to the House of Commons on August 20, 1940, Mr. Churchill had predicted that "the British Empire and the United States will have to be somewhat mixed up together in some of their affairs for mutual and general advantage." Evidently the mixing is to be one of resources, not of constitutions.

Both in the political and in the economic sphere the benefits at which the President and Mr. Churchill aim are universal in scope, and the method by which they are to be attained is the nearest possible approach to universal voluntary co-operation. When the time comes for carrying these intentions into effect, the necessity of organization (provisional perhaps but none the less effective) will be apparent at an early stage. If it is to bear any relation to the Declaration of the Atlantic, that organization cannot be a limited union; it must be a world-wide association.

A world association binding together and co-ordinating regional groupings of states may evolve toward one universal federal government, as in the past loose confederations have grown into federal unions. Such evolution will bring with it increasing security of peace and social progress. World government is the ultimate aim; but there is more chance of attaining it by gradual development than by attempting to join discordant elements in an immediately perfect constitution.

CHAPTER IX

LAW AND THE COMMUNITY OF STATES

In time of peace states observe certain widely accepted principles in their dealings with each other and with each other's citizens. The modes in which new territory is acquired, either by transfer from one state to another or by discovery and settlement; the rights and duties of states in relation to foreigners resident on their soil; control over ships at sea, in coastal waters and in harbors; the privileges of ambassadors; international aviation—these and many other matters are regulated by a body of rules growing out of custom, set by treaty, or adopted from the treatises of jurists, and commonly known as international law or law of nations.

Thus in some respects the position of the state is like that of the individual human being in the political community. When it considers that its rights have been violated by another state, it protests and asks for compensation. If redress is refused, resort is often had to arbitration by some person or body agreed upon by the two parties to the dispute. The arbitration ends in an award very similar to the judgment of a court, and the losing state is often called upon to pay damages. In the last century and a half this mode of settling international disputes has become increasingly common, and the cases in which states have refused to comply with an award are remarkably few. The practice of arbitration, and the creation of the Permanent Court of Arbitration and the Permanent Court of International Justice in 1899 and 1922, respectively, at The Hague, are part of the evidence of a growing recognition that the states of the world together form a community and are subject to the law established in that community.

Until 1928, however, international law did not prohibit war. It did not even attempt to limit the occasions on which war might legally be resorted to. It did contain many rules, some of them established by long practice, others by great law-making conferences like those held at The Hague in 1899 and 1907, which were intended to limit the methods of warfare. It also tried to control the conduct of belligerents toward neutrals, limiting particularly the right of interference with neutral trade. But when wars actually broke out, many of these rules were disregarded by states driven to adopt every available means of winning a victory. Poison gas was used, open towns were bombarded, civilian populations were maltreated, hospitals were bombed, hospital ships sunk. Neutral shipping was captured or sent to the bottom and neutral goods confiscated by unprecedented extensions of blockade and contraband. The painfully compiled codes of "civilized warfare" were of little avail. Scarcely any offense was too revolting to be justified as retaliation for an alleged previous breach by the enemy.

The fact that states could legalize any kind of extortion by declaring war, and the brutal violations of the "laws of war," brought international law into popular contempt. Manifestations of unbridled violence were so spectacular, and caused such suffering to masses of people, that the layman was apt to ignore the fact that even in the midst of war the rules of international law were regulating the daily and hourly intercourse of the nations still at peace, and that but for such rules there would be no order at all in international relations.

The layman was not alone in his contempt for the so-called law of nations. Many lawyers despised it because it was unsupported by any organized community force. Technically speaking, it had none of the sure "sanctions" that normally fall on those persons who violate the law of the state. They said that it wasn't, properly speaking, law at all.

Certainly a system of rules which does not forbid a state to use violence to procure something which it cannot get by peaceful means fails in one of the principal purposes of law, which is to eliminate violence from society. Certainly also, a system which has behind it no organized power for its enforcement is weak to the point where its description as law becomes dubious.

The Briand-Kellogg Pact of 1928 was an attempt to remedy the first of these defects. That agreement was ratified by sixty-two states, including all the Great Powers, and in it the parties renounced war as an instrument of national policy and undertook never to seek except by peaceful means the solution of any dispute between them. The notes and discussions accompanying the negotiation and ratification of the pact indicate quite clearly that war in self-defense was not understood to be prohibited. This in itself would not have been a fault. Even the most perfect national law allows a man to fend off an assault by force. For practical purposes the defect in the position achieved by the treaty was that states were left to judge for themselves what constituted self-defense.

This is a defect of the whole international legal system. There is no court with authority over every member of the community of states, no court before which a state that has suffered violence can hale the assailant and make him prove that his act was in self-defense or pay the penalty for an assault. Even the Permanent Court of International Justice, which has made the furthest advance in this direction, has authority only over those states which have accepted its jurisdiction.

To have practical effect, a rule which limits war to self-defense must have behind it a court with authority to define the limits of self-defense in every case and to impose a penalty for violence not falling within that definition.

The other great weakness of the international legal system, namely that there is no world police to enforce its rules, is still without so much as a remedy on paper. It means, among other things, that even the judgment of an international court has to depend for fulfillment on the good will of the loser or the power of the winner. It is a rule of international law that if a state has submitted to arbitration it must fulfill the award, but that rule may be disregarded with the same impunity as any other. True, the moral disapproval of the world may be a little more profound and outspoken, but the world has not provided machinery for enforcement. Perhaps the chief reason why the awards and judgments of international courts have so infrequently been disregarded is that powerful states have hitherto held back from arbitration, as "political" or "nonlegal" disputes, cases in which they feel a vital interest. In matters of minor importance they have been willing to take the chance of losing and to obey an unfavorable decision. Anything like secure justice as between nations would require power, lodged in an agency of the world community, and capable, at need, of compelling even a great state first to submit any dispute, however important, to arbitral or judicial decision, and then to comply with judgment.

The two defects are obviously closely related. If war is to be effectively outlawed, there must not only be courts with authority to define the limits of self-defense and condemn the transgressor, but organized force ready for the prevention of violence and for the execution of judicial decrees.

A third imperfection in the international legal system has been the lack of a universal legislature with authority to change rules that have fallen out of date and become an obstacle to reasonable progress. The law of the modern state is under constant revision to prevent it from shackling scientific, technical and social advancement, even to make of it, instead, an active instrument of reform. One of the excuses for continuing to recognize war as a legal institution has been the absence, in the community of states, of any other effective instrumentality of change. Since there is no body to which states can refer situations that have become inequitable, though in accordance with existing rules, it is argued that they are justified in making the needed change by their own strength. Conferences are an imperfect substitute because, in the prevailing theory, no state is considered bound by any convention to which it has not agreed. Old law cannot therefore be changed or new law added save by unanimous consent, and it is naturally difficult to persuade states benefiting by the existing inequitable situation to agree to its alteration.

Some of these, it may be objected, are defects in the administration and development of the law rather than in the law itself; and they have been dealt with in some detail among the problems of constitutional machinery. But constitutional machinery is part and parcel of the law and its imperfections may be a direct consequence of underlying legal doctrine. For purposes of general information it would be futile to discuss the weaknesses of the basic principles of the contemporary law of nations without connecting them with the most visible of their practical manifestations.

The Covenant of the League of Nations, the charter of the International Labor Organization, and the Statute of the Permanent Court of International Justice, were all attempts to remedy the constitutional machinery of the community of states without altering the fundamental theory of international law. That is one way of stating the reasons for the failure of these institutions to keep the peace.

Thus the Covenant tried, by providing machinery for the settlement of disputes, to make less common the resort to war. It even devised (Article 19) a voluntary procedure for the revision of treaties and the "consideration of international conditions whose continuance might endanger the peace of the world." But it did not make war illegal or declare that states must submit to the reform of inequitable situations. It provided economic sanctions against states resorting to war in violation of Covenanted obligations; but it left members of the League free to judge for themselves whether such violation had occurred and whether, therefore, they were under any duty to cut off commercial and financial relations with the accused state. As for military sanctions, there was no pretense of making these automatic or compulsory.

Part XIII of the Treaty of Versailles established what was in many ways an admirable procedure for the equalization and amelioration of labor conditions, but it did not attempt to make the draft conventions of the International Labor

Conferences binding on states that refused to ratify them. The Statute of the Permanent Court of International Justice achieved what previous attempts had failed to accomplish, namely an acceptable way of constituting a judicial tribunal open to all states; but it did not confer compulsory jurisdiction on this tribunal.

At every point these constitutional arrangements abstained from infringing a fixed principle in the prevailing doctrine of international law, namely the sovereignty of the state. That doctrine was deeply ingrained in the minds of governments and jurists and had much to do with the unwillingness of the conference to construct institutions with the power of direct action. To have done so would have been to override the historic claim of the state to independence from all external compulsion.

This refusal would almost certainly have been justified, if reasons had been demanded, by the assertion that it expressed the will of the peoples represented. The fault, then, of the governments and their delegates and advisers was that they either did not realize the impossibility of preserving intact the alleged sovereignty of the state and at the same time setting up the institutions of an effective community of nations, or that they failed to explain this impossibility to their peoples and ask for a clear-cut choice between restitution of the *status quo*, on the one hand, and the inauguration of a really new era on the other. Instead, they set up a building with an imposing façade and very little foundation.

It has been a long and costly deception to assert the existence of international law and at the same time to deny that the state is bound by any rule to which it has not given its explicit or implied consent; to declare that states owe obedience to international law but to maintain that they are themselves judges of what the law is and what constitutes obedience to it, and may always legally refuse to submit such questions to impartial decision; to talk of a law binding upon nations but to insist that where it appears to conflict with the law of the state the courts and officials of the state must apply the latter; and finally to pay lip service to an international legal system while admitting that any violation of another's acknowledged right may be legalized by a declaration of war.

Here, then, are some of the amendments in fundamental principles which must be introduced if law is ever to become a reasonably secure guaranty of order in international affairs.

First it must be recognized that the law of nations takes precedence over national law, and consequently that no alleged law of a state is really law at all if it conflicts with a rule of the international system. Thus the law of nations may become what it must be if it is to be effective—a supranational law. Sovereignty would then mean only that measure of autonomy which supranational law leaves to the state. This change in the theory of the state and the world community, it is almost needless to say, will not be made unless the governments and their legal advisers are given to believe that their peoples demand the abandonment of all that claim to arbitrary national discretion which has been a perpetual source of conflict. If the national groups are unwilling to give up a discretion which is incompatible with any real community, there cannot be any secure legal order in the world at large.

Secondly, as in every civilized national system of law, it must be established as a rule of supranational law that a state called upon to refer a dispute to impartial decision is bound to do so. This change of theory can only produce its effects in practice if there are suitable tribunals before which a state cannot legally refuse to go. Here the ground is already broken. But when the Permanent Court of International Justice is restored to its place and function, its jurisdiction must be made compulsory within the range of matters assigned to it. There is much to be said also for constituting it a Supreme World Court, with appeal in certain cases from regional tribunals more easily accessible to litigants. Such regionalization would also improve the chances of enforcing judgments when necessary; for there is evidence in the history of the League of Nations that the use of organized force to compel obedience to the law is more practicable in limited areas than on a universal scale.

Peaceful change to take the place of war also involves not only the provision of new machinery but drastic amendment of basic theory as well. The institutional structure necessary for this purpose is discussed in later chapters. Here it will suffice to point out that the amendment of old law and the creation of new—in a word the legislative function—implies majority decision. Unanimity, which means a free veto for every member of the community of states, has not totally prevented progress but has made it too slow to keep up with changing needs. If we want an adequate substitute for violence as an instrument of change, we are therefore once more face to face with the necessity of cutting down the doctrine of sovereignty to the proportions of the liberty of the individual in the state.

What is being asked for here is nothing more nor less than one detail in a general reorientation of legal theory—a change in the dominant attitude of governments, legislators, and lawyers. The reality of the supranational community must be incorporated in legal doctrine as one of those general principles of law valid everywhere. Looked at from this point of view the existing law of nations reveals its defects and inconsistencies in high relief. Hitherto international law has been at the best an attempt to achieve a principle of social order while preserving in theoretical absoluteness the independence of the state. The result has been a congeries of precepts with so little internal cohesion, so many conflicts, that, while they served a useful purpose under peaceful conditions, they did not provide a clear barrier even of doctrine against ruthless and powerful interest. To construct community institutions without fundamental reform in the legal theory of the community would be like setting out to build a house upon plans designed for rapid collapse rather than enduring resistance to strains.

Hitherto international law has not given any rights directly to the individual human being. If the individual is injured by the failure of a foreign state to fulfill a duty imposed upon it by the law of nations, he must seek redress through his own state. The prevailing legal view has been that the right infringed in such cases is not one belonging to the individual, but is the right of his state to have its nationals treated according to certain standards by other states. Even where tribunals have been set up by agreement to deal with claims like these, recourse to them has usually been limited to the states themselves, who must adopt their national's claim as their own before it can be submitted for adjudication. This has meant difficult complications for the sufferer and delays in obtaining justice which have often reached fantastic lengths. Opposition to the admission of the individual in his own right before such bodies proceeds again from the concept of the sovereignty and majesty of the state, which must not be exposed to question by anything less than another state. The excuse commonly offered, however, is the alleged necessity of guarding international tribunals from frivolous or excessively numerous applications. Why they need such protection more than national courts has not been made clear. If they do, it might easily be provided by a rule requiring a summary preliminary scrutiny by an official of the claimant's state, designed solely to ascertain that there is serious evidence of a grievance.

In the Mixed Arbitral Tribunals set up in 1919 to deal with claims arising out of the war of 1914-1918, in the International Joint Commission between the United States and Canada, and in some other limited arbitral arrangements, the individual has been allowed to appear as party in his own right, and there is reason to believe that these precedents will be followed. We may hope, therefore, that at least where the individual suffers injury at the hands of a foreign community, he will be admitted to have a direct right of redress.

What now of redress against oppression by his own state? Further difficulty confronts the reform, advocated by an increasing number of internationalists, which would establish liberty of speech, information, association, and religion as rights of every human being under supranational law. To us who live under democratic government, such an advance seems highly desirable. But it involves a severe limitation upon the authority of the state over its own nationals. Has the demand for universal social progress which is being stimulated by the present war taken this into account, and will it reach such revolutionary power?

CHAPTER X

SOVEREIGNTY AND NATIONALISM VERSUS THE COMMUNITY OF STATES

We have seen that one principal reason assigned for the failure of the League of Nations was the lack of means at its direct disposal for the enforcement of its decisions. Save in matters of procedure and some rare cases specified in the Covenant, the decisions themselves, whether of Council or Assembly, required a unanimous vote of the members present. This was simply a general expression of the reservation of the sovereignty of the states belonging to the League. To make the reservation doubly sure, interpretations and practice supported the claim of any state to decide for itself, even after a decision in Council or Assembly, whether it would take part in the most important tasks which the League was designed to perform.

Such cautious restrictions were loud evidence of the fact that the most destructive war in human history had not been enough to convince the world's politicians that the state must be subordinated to the international community. A constant note in the deliberations of Council and Assembly was that the League was a co-operative organization, not a superstate. Far from setting up a real central authority and endowing it with the right and the means of controlling by its own motion the conduct of recalcitrant states, the Covenant did little more, for the most serious purposes, than set up institutions through which the members could take joint action if they so desired. Such at least was the interpretation put upon that document by resolution and accumulating precedent.

Even if the Covenant had been interpreted as endowing the organs of the League with powers of decision binding on its members, these organs had clearly not been given the means of execution. The League had no power to impose a direct economic blockade; still less had it the right, the men, or the arms, to take measures involving physical force. Any sequel to decision depended on the concordant action of the individual states.

The reason for this exhibition of eating the cake and having it, of building a "new world" without making place for it by clearing away the debris of the old, was that mankind, or at least the political representatives of mankind, still believed that the state was the highest possible concentration of authority under heaven. The delegates at Versailles were pledged to give visible form to a growing sense of interdependence, to make a working reality of a vaguely perceived world community. They fulfilled their promise by setting up the forms of a great society and refusing to give them the vital force which alone could make the new institutions operate. Within this framework they built new states, endowing them with the absolutism which, whether or not they realized it, had to be eradicated in those that already existed if any international organization was to succeed. Because they had not understood, or at any rate not acted upon, this essential truth, the League which they founded was destined to aggravate rather than alleviate the clash of nationalisms.

There are two aspects of sovereignty, one of which is still useful while the other has become a principle of chaos. Only the anarchist quarrels with the view that human life is enhanced by the government, under central authority, of groups formed by that complex of geographic, economic, biologic and cultural factors which we bundle together under the vague term of nationhood. But this legitimate, internal aspect of sovereignty has for centuries been coupled with a fallacious corollary which makes of the organized nation, that is to say the state, an entity independent of all external control. As a doctrine that served a useful purpose in breaking down the claims of the Papacy or the Holy Roman Empire to impose an arbitrary direction from outside upon the organized national group, the alleged external sovereignty of the state won for itself a more than religious awe. Wrapped in a protective sheath of mysticism, it outlived its usefulness and became a major obstacle to the growth of an effective law of nations. At the same time it prevented the creation of those superstate institutions which the philosophers of the Renaissance already perceived to be necessary for the preservation of peace and the advancement of human welfare.

Thus, having served to destroy competing central authorities which were undesirable because they had no reference to the majority will of the subject groups, the doctrine of sovereignty in its external aspect has prevented the erection of a supranational authority established by the majority will of the world community and continuously responsive to that will. The Nazi philosophy, conscious of the havoc wreaked by a multitude of sovereignties, proposes to return to the medieval unity of Europe, this time under a German Empire free of the papal competition which limited its Holy Roman prototype. This imposed unification is of course designed to serve the interests of a supreme German race, rather than of Europe, and it is to be the antithesis in method and spirit of a constitutionally governed democracy. It will not mean abandonment of national sovereignty, only the forced subordination of all governments to one; not the establishment of a European community under shared authority and taking its place in a recognized world community, only the domination of a European mass by one deified sovereign state in perpetual and ungoverned competition with other states.

If it were merely a doctrine of constitutionalists, or a rule of action for foreign offices, the theory of sovereignty which makes the state judge in its own cause and in all matters of "vital interest" a law unto itself might perhaps have been abandoned long ago in the face of popular resistance to its consequences. But the poet and the politician have combined to give the legal formula its explosive popular embodiment in patriotism or nationalism. It would be difficult of course to conceive of a better guide for conduct than enlightened patriotism; but in the form of nationalism—the apotheosis of the group interest, devotion to "my country, right or wrong"—the virtue is transmuted into one of the great evils of our day.

Nationalism is conceded to be one of the strongest of contemporary political forces, and it threatens to be a continuing obstacle to general progress. Whether it is altogether a spontaneous emotion arising naturally and inevitably from kinship and neighborhood, or is in considerable measure the artificial product of propaganda, is a question of some importance. To the extent that it results from stimulation by parties interested in using the power of the nation for purposes which they determine, it may be controlled—even turned to the use of the international community—by measures applied to those parties, who are relatively few in number and therefore more accessible than the national mass. It may be impossible to "indict a whole people" but quite possible to indict and to coerce, when necessary, its leaders. On analysis, nationalism as a force opposing the implementation of the world-community may therefore prove less primeval and less massive than is commonly supposed.

Of late years the doctrine of sovereignty and the exaggerated nationalism which is its popular counterpart have come in for multilateral attack. The economists have shown the unreality of national independence in industrial, commercial and financial policy; the sociologists of the League and International Labor Organization have revealed the extent to which physical and moral health, together with the conditions of life and labor, are determined by forces that disregard frontiers; while jurists are turning away from a theory of international law built upon the legal supremacy of the state to one which accepts the subordination of national juridical systems to the law of nations.

These attacks have not dislodged national sovereignty from its place as the doctrine determining the conduct of foreign offices and the governments behind them, or deflated nationalism as a popular summons to conflict. The appeal to reason is still weaker than the appeal to prejudice and emotion, and the latter therefore continues to be preferred by the politician. Diplomacy also clings to the fetish, partly because it is familiar and partly because the reduction of the state to its proper place in the human community would deprive the diplomatic art of a large part of its pomp and circumstance.

The result, as the interests of nations have become more and more interwoven, has been an increasing discrepancy between the theory of the state and the facts of human life. The state, as that institution has been traditionally understood, is easily proved to be a thoroughly inefficient instrument of man's welfare. It is inefficient because it has not been geared to run smoothly as portion of a universal mechanism designed to serve interests which cannot be broken up in national compartments. This discrepancy and inefficiency are prominent among the causes of war and poverty.

Such is the almost unanimous refrain of our writers and orators on the organization of peace. Almost without exception they postulate the "sacrifice" of important aspects of national sovereignty in the form of a transfer to supranational authority of rights and powers hitherto regarded as the prerogative of states. For much the greater part, what is involved is a "sacrifice" of illusions; since the capacity to carry into practice this theoretical prerogative could never (precisely because it is absolute) belong to more than one state at a time.

The success of any new organization for peace, whether it take the form merely of federal union in Europe, or of a series of regional associations linked together in a revived and reformed League, presupposes clear realization on the part of governments and peoples that the state is being subordinated to a larger community. That means not only a drastic change in legal theory but at the same time a shifting of loyalty. In all matters of universal concern the obedience of the official and private individual must be transferred from the national government to the supranational authority. The state must cease to be the final arbiter of conduct.

The change in legal theory is of prime importance. Even in the democratic countries most ostensibly devoted to peace and the establishment of the rule of law among nations, the legal rule still obtains that the highest tribunal must declare any statutory enactment of the national legislature to be law, regardless of its conflict with international law, and that the highest executive must carry into effect the law so declared. This is true of Great Britain and the United States today. In other words, the primacy of national over international law is part of the constitution, written or unwritten. It is part of the training of lawyers, the group who advise foreign offices and form the largest element in legislatures and governments. The theory must be explicitly and unmistakably reversed.

One of the taproots of nationalism will thus be severed. Steps will then need to be taken to stop the preaching of the supremacy of the state. Thus a beginning may be made in the process of shifting part at least of the allegiance of the mass to the supranational community. The process will have to be assisted by the deletion of the nationalistic material employed in educational textbooks and its replacement by material explaining the benefits of wider association. More general training in elementary economics might well serve this positive purpose, for this would reveal the folly of setting the apparent interest of the nation over that of mankind.

What cries out for understanding is that modern technology and business organization have woven humanity into a community. Man's political organization still lags behind, kicking against the pricks that urge it forward. By little and little the unescapable fact of community finds expression in agencies of administration that operate with delegated powers over an area that is world-wide. Each of these is a step in the equipment of a world society which must eventually control the action of the individual state in every matter that produces substantial effects outside its borders.

Meanwhile the formula of sovereignty and the artificially nurtured emotion of nationalism continue to impede man's rational adjustment to his changed environment.

The nation-state was itself formed by the fusion of family and clan groups, a gradual political development taking place in slow response to intensifying social and economic relationships between the groups. Such is the process of political evolution, the gradual recognition of the need of unified authority over ever wider groups and areas. At times the current has been reversed, as it was by the fractioning of authority under the feudal system. But the re-subordination of the fiefs to central monarchies is an exact prototype of the process of regional and world organization which set in before the end of the nineteenth century with the establishment of institutions like the Universal Telegraph and Postal Unions, and which has gathered speed in the twentieth century. We are in the stage of transition from the nation-state to a world community.

The transition is impeded by vested political interest, and violently disturbed by the urgent ambitions of demagogues. So was the transition from the family or feudal group to the nation-state. But just as the latter development was assisted by the establishment of fragments of state organization, around which a larger loyalty was able to grow, so the movement toward the world community will gain support as each new institution provides a visible symbol of unity. In the light of political history it would seem that the question is not so much whether this larger integration will take place as how much time it will require. Must it await the slow conviction of haphazard and prolonged trial and error, or can it be hastened by planning based upon our knowledge of the nature and working of political institutions? This book, like the numerous studies summarized in earlier chapters, is devoted to the thesis that human intelligence is sufficiently advanced to shorten, in the construction of the world community, the long process of piecemeal organization that resulted in the nation-state. The **League of Nations, a compromise faulty in itself and soon** abandoned by the shortsighted policy of the states which founded it, was yet able to achieve enough of lasting value to support this view, which is further confirmed by the work of the related International Labor Organization, and by the success, in the judicial sphere, of that offspring of the League, the Permanent Court of International Justice.

CHAPTER XI

ECONOMIC AND FINANCIAL ORGANIZATION[1]

Peace and the satisfaction of man's material wants are so intimately connected that it is not far from equally true to say that no lasting peace can be hoped for so long as large masses of people suffer or fear recurrent privation, and to say that recurrent privation is inevitable so long as wars are allowed to happen. Hitherto attempts to organize peace have emphasized the political motif, concentrating on the construction of machinery to settle disputes and prevent aggression in the belief that, given order and security, economic relations would look after themselves. The economic organization of the League of Nations was of a fact-finding and advisory nature with no power of decision and execution. Since the League failed to keep the peace, there is now a marked tendency to insist that ways and means of heightening standards of living must occupy the forefront of any new effort at world organization.

This approach to the problem of peace, being partly a reaction against the too "political" or "formal" character of the League, is apt to obscure the importance of non-economic factors in international politics and to become as defectively one-sided as the dominantly political approach. It may be taken as demonstrated, however, that the community of states must devise means of preventing or mitigating major inequities and major disturbances in the distribution of goods. Men will fight if, rightly or wrongly, they are persuaded that they cannot otherwise win food, clothing and shelter. Nor is it any longer to be taken for granted, as it was in the nineteenth century, that welfare will follow automatically on security from military disturbance.

[1] In this chapter I have had the benefit of personal consultation with Professor J. B. Condliffe and Professor Eugene Staley, whose writings are frequently cited in the text, and have been further assisted by W. L. Holland, Research Secretary of the Institute of Pacific Relations. With this grateful acknowledgment, I remain solely responsible for the contents.

By setting up a supranational authority with power enough to prevent physical aggression, we may secure states against invasion. But unless at the same time we establish agencies to regulate economic relations, those same states may be impoverished by monopolistic policies on the part of economically strong neighbors. They will then seek to undermine the anti-aggression system and, if they can muster the strength for it, will take violent means of getting what they have been denied.

Before the war of 1914-18, the production and exchange of goods and services within states, and the interchange of goods and services between them, was left in the main to private initiative. There were of course in various countries state monopolies of some commodities, state-owned systems of transportation and communication, and public utilities owned and operated by states and municipalities. Private ownership and enterprise were however the dominant principles in the world at large. The producer of food, raw materials, or manufactured articles, sold his product where he could get the highest price, the manufacturer and the consumer bought where they could buy most cheaply. Shipping, insurance, and financial services, provided by private individuals or firms, were directed to any place, regardless of boundaries, where they could make adequate earnings.

Tariffs imposed by governments, either for revenue purposes or to protect national producers against foreign competition, interfered to some extent with the movement of commodities across national boundaries; but such checks were for the most part temporary in nature, if only because price-advances in the protected market or decreased production costs in the exporting country in time neutralized the deterrent effect of customs duties. Legislative restrictions on the quantity of imports, control over the purchase of foreign money with which to pay for imported goods, and clearing arrangements limiting the flow of international trade and directing it to specific countries, were practically unknown.

Similarly the investor placed his money where it would

earn the highest return. The free movement of capital opened up new sources of food and raw materials, stimulated industrial development in virgin territory and, by creating purchasing power in the receiving countries, expanded the market for manufactured goods.

Labor also sought the highest market. Free migration relieved population pressure at home, and the immigrants' earnings, whether spent in the new country or sent back home, increased the demand for consumer goods. Already there were barriers against the black and yellow races, but the American nations held wide their doors to the human surplus of Europe.

In all of this movement and exchange, England, the British navy, and the London money-market played a pre-eminent role. As a great manufacturing country with a population far in excess of the domestic food supply, Great Britain offered a vast market, unguarded by tariffs, for European and overseas food and raw materials. Her naval supremacy enabled her to maintain something approaching a balance of power in Europe and to exercise a pacifying influence in the Near and Far East. Wars were, if not rare, at any rate limited in geographical extent and of short duration. Traders, investors, contractors could have a fair measure of confidence that their transactions would not be cut off by hostilities. The accumulated profits of the English industrial revolution and its sequel flowed through the "City" to every part of the world where good dividends and reasonable security offered. English ships were the world's carriers. London was the great source of loans, governmental and private, the creator and controller of commercial credit, the universal bill-broker.

The gold standard operated as a simple and automatic device for keeping the principal currencies—pounds, dollars, francs and marks—in a steady ratio of value one to the other. If the demand for dollars to pay for an excess of imports to England over exports and services to the United States raised the price of the dollar in terms of the pound, the English debtor purchased gold in England and, instead of paying his American creditor in dollars, paid him by shipping the gold to the United States. Thus, so long as the banks sold gold at the same rate in the national currency, fluctuations in exchange rates were limited to the margin at which it became profitable to pay the expenses of shipping gold.

The relatively free competition of alternative sources of supply, coupled with the working of the gold standard, tended to prevent wide or rapid fluctuations of price. The purchaser could tell over a considerable period and in terms of his own currency what he would have to pay for the foreign goods that he needed; while the producer knew what he would get for his product. Sudden shifts might occur, particularly in agricultural commodities subject to weather conditions. There were also occasional general depressions. The major trend, however, was a fairly even rise in the volume of international trade and financial transactions.

The war of 1914-18 transferred the largest possible portion of national productive capacities from goods for peaceful uses at home or abroad to arms and munitions. It destroyed vast quantities of productive plant, and sank much of the world's shipping. It cut off established channels of trade. It heaped unprecedented debts on the belligerents, and the service of these debts deflected money from the restoration and development of production. It created a congeries of new states with tariff walls where none had previously existed. In its wake followed famine, revolution, unemployment. The huge task of reconstruction, and of transition from a war economy to one of peace, was complicated by uneconomic boundaries and by an impossible burden of reparations. England, overtaxed by her own needs of reconstruction and readaptation, and gradually forced into default on her war debt to the United States, was in no position to extend the loans and credits which had formerly oiled the wheels of world commerce. Her most important European market, in Germany, was destroyed; and her greatest industries faced a long period of depression. Runaway currency depreciations on the Continent, contrasting with the "City's" drive to restore the pound to its prewar parity with the dollar, put a prohibitive price on English manufactures. Markets not shut off in this way were rendered difficult of access by rising tariff walls. The United States, whose new position as the greatest creditor nation should have dictated a low-tariff policy to permit payment (since in the long run debts can only be paid in goods or services) was a chief sinner in this respect. The sharp rise in the American tariff in 1922 was "the first heavy blow directed against any hope of effectively restoring a world trading system."[2]

The League of Nations was not equipped to restore order in the economic chaos resulting from the war. At intervals from 1920 on it held conferences designed to reveal and to remove the causes of the more immediate strains, and to define the principles of general recovery. It raised loans and directed their application to the relief of Austria and Hungary, hardest hit of the European states by the dislocations of the war and its sequels. It tried to mitigate the effects of rising tariffs by drafting conventions for the simplification and publication of customs rates and formalities. Its economists warned of the dangers involved in import and export prohibitions. But it had neither the legal authority nor the financial resources to offer or impose, of its own volition, remedies for the disastrous fall in international trade.

In 1925 the Dawes Plan, with its revision of the scale and method of reparations payments, and its sequel of loans to Germany, brought a marked improvement in international relations, political and economic. France's withdrawal from the Ruhr, the Locarno guaranties, and the arrangements for the admission of Germany to the League, reinforced this improved trend. Floated on a fresh stream of capital from the United States, a mounting volume of international trade moved over the barriers erected by nations in the effort to lift themselves by their own bootstraps. One country after another returned to the gold

[2] J. B. Condliffe, *The Reconstruction of World Trade*, p. 182.

standard, and a relative stability in the principal currencies was thus achieved. The stabilization of the pound at prewar parity with the dollar, in 1925, was indeed a sacrifice of industry to finance which, by keeping English costs at too high a level, impeded sound recovery—a weak spot in the foundations of the whole international structure which contributed much to the subsequent collapse.

Another serious weak point in the upward movement from 1925 to 1929 was the shrinking price of agricultural commodities and the accumulation of agricultural surpluses. This was the result of encouragement, through tariffs and subsidies, of agricultural production in various European countries which, partly to avoid the immediate cost of importing and partly with the political motive of independence from external sources of supply, sought self-sufficiency. The overseas producers, principally debtor countries, saw their normal means of payment vanishing and could avoid default and continue production only by further loans. The general effect was, however, more fundamental. One of the basic operations of international trade, the exchange of food for manufactured articles, was thrown out of gear.

Foreign markets for manufactured goods were also narrowing. It could hardly be otherwise, given the devaluation of agricultural products. But here also the ill-guided urge toward self-sufficiency, prompted partly by short-term economic considerations and partly by political motives, produced its evil effects. Almost everywhere industrial as well as agricultural tariffs were rising.

It was credit expansion, and a huge development in capital goods, especially in the United States but in Europe, Asia and South America as well, that explained the increase in international trade in defiance of soaring tariffs. The movement was artificial and unsound. The upward trend continued precisely as long as the somewhat reckless outpouring of loans and credits from the United States. That came to a sudden halt in the panic of 1929. The funds from which Germany and other debtor countries in Europe and elsewhere had been serving their debts and financing expanding production dried up. There was no longer the wherewithal to administer artificial stimulants or to conceal underlying weakness.

The inevitable collapse in Europe was averted for a time by official moratoria and by accommodations between national banks. The crash of the Austrian Credit-Anstalt in May 1931, marked the limit of these palliatives. That was followed by the temporary ruin of the entire German banking system; and financial crisis spread over Europe. Withdrawal of short-term funds from London forced Britain off the gold standard in September 1931. In its fall, sterling carried with it the currencies of the many countries whose economies depended chiefly upon the English market. A new period of exchange instability set in. Industrial development ceased as the drying up of the sources of fresh loans was followed by the withdrawal of old capital to safer havens. Default followed default in international debts.

In 1930 the United States, greatest of creditor nations, had emphasized by the Smoot-Hawley tariff its unwillingness to accept foreign goods in payment. Partly in retaliation, the British Commonwealth transformed itself into a closed trading corporation by the introduction of the United Kingdom tariff of 1931 and the system of preferences established in the Ottawa Agreements of 1932. Everywhere governments adopted new devices for preserving national financial resources and safeguarding the home market for national producers. Fresh barriers far more effective than tariffs were erected in the channels of international trade. Import quotas, governmental limitation and control of the purchase of foreign exchange, barter and clearing arrangements eliminating the use of money, spread from one country to another.

The general effect of these devices is well described in the report on International Economic Reconstruction completed at the end of 1937 by M. Paul van Zeeland, former Prime Minister of Belgium. "The isolated, divergent, and contradictory measures by which the nations, in the first period of the late crisis, attempted to protect themselves against it and push off the burden on their neighbors only served to precipitate it and to render it yet more grievous for all."[3]

The Nazi regime in Germany rose to power and consolidated itself as the result, in large part, of the rising wave of unemployment and general economic distress. By a rapid and immense development of the armament industries it provided employment, the necessary foreign materials being procured by barter arrangements and a ruthless drive for export markets. Internally and externally the entire economic activity of the German people was organized in such a way as to build up an unprecedented equipment for the war which was to end, by territorial expansion, the present poverty and present sacrifices of Germany.

The increasing sense of political insecurity in face of the rising power of Germany was partly responsible for the recovery movement that was already visible in 1933 and continued until 1937. The movement indeed began from other causes and between those countries which had lagged behind in the crescendo of restriction and control. Even so, it was an astonishing demonstration of the ingenuity of private traders in surmounting the obstacles erected by public policy. In its later stages, however, it was largely a reflection of the scramble for raw materials needed in the general rearmament touched off by Hitler.[4] As the political situation deteriorated, and the threatening and threatened nations strove to strengthen their immediate financial and industrial position for the forthcoming struggle, neither human ingenuity nor the demand for raw materials could outweigh the throttling effect of cumulative restrictions, and trade again fell off.

The Second World War broke upon a world in which one mode of international economic life, resting upon the free movement of goods, capital and labor, had been utterly destroyed, and no alternative system had been created. More

[3] From the text in *International Conciliation*, No. 338, March 1938, p. 83.
[4] Condliffe, *op. cit.*, pp. 134-135.

and more people have come to understand that the breakdown was in a considerable measure the result of the war of 1914-18 and that it is at least partly responsible for the war of 1939. If it is true that we cannot afford wars, it is also true that we cannot risk prolonged economic depressions. President Roosevelt and Mr. Anthony Eden are agreed that the post-war world must be one in which men shall be free from want. Both in the days when the new war-clouds were gathering, and now when destruction blazes in Europe, Africa and Asia, economists, political scientists and international lawyers have been devoting themselves to the study of ways and means for building such a world. How is that to be done? By restoring the *laisser faire* doctrine and practice which prevailed in the nineteenth century and the first decade of the twentieth, by organizing on a supranational plane the desirable exchange between nations, or by a mixture of *laisser faire* and organized control?

Governments will neither desire nor be permitted to surrender all of the controls which they have assumed in recent years.[5] At a very minimum, regulation of the hours and conditions of labor, including wages, has come to stay; and that necessarily involves far-reaching intervention in economic processes. The state will also continue to regard itself as responsible for preventing destitution and keeping employment at a high level. This cannot but mean active supervision of the fortunes of the various industries, with encouragement of some and limitation of others as demand and costs change. The great problem will be how to maintain an intelligent direction, avoiding national restrictions which, for an immediate economic advantage or for purposes of political aggrandizement, inflict disproportionate damage upon other nations and destroy a generally profitable interchange of goods and services. Such direction cannot be expected if states are left free to choose, in complete sovereignty, their own policies.

[5] *Cf.* the van Zeeland Report, *loc. cit.*, p. 102, and M. J. Bonn, "The New World Order," *Annals of the American Academy of Political and Social Science*, July 1941, p. 173.

It is useless, then, to look to a restoration of nineteenth century conditions for our economic salvation. The vast and intricate network of cross-boundary exchanges, resting on private initiative and the free movement of goods, capital and labor, was responsible for the greatest advance that history has seen in the standards of living. The period of *laisser faire* was also, as it happens, the longest stretch of comparative peace that man has known. But the whole structure was built around a Great Britain pre-eminent in industrial development, financial resources and capacity, and in naval power. It depended, moreover, on a separation of politics and economics and an inequality of privilege that men are not likely again to tolerate.

The benevolent economic dictatorship of England was an essential part of that nineteenth century situation which "could not last in face of the developing industrial power of late comers in the international arena."[6] It is unlikely that any single Power can again hold such a position, even though the United States with its increasing superiority of economic and military strength were willing to assume the role of sole leadership. Nations can hardly be expected to abandon their policies of control in favor of dependence on the hazards of voluntary benevolence. Under existing conditions even a combination of two or more principal Powers in a joint dictatorship with the most liberal motives would be at least as apt to provoke rival combinations as grateful co-operation.

If we cannot or would not return to general *laisser faire*, under the *de facto* supremacy of one or two Powers, and yet see nothing but permanent disaster if the present trend of unco-ordinated unilateral control persists, only one course remains open, namely that of international or (more accurately) supranational co-ordination. This is the conclusion accepted by such economists as Professor Eugene Staley in his *World Economy in Transition*, J. E. Meade in his *Economic Analysis and Policy* and *Economic Bases of a Durable Peace*, and, with more emphasis on the difficulties and less

[6] Condliffe, *op. cit.*, pp. 51-52.

confidence of success, Professor Condliffe in *The Reconstruction of World Trade*.

Professor Staley's *World Economy in Transition* demonstrates with vivid examples how modern industrial techniques have created an insatiable demand for new raw materials. No country has anything like the entire range within its own borders. Technological progress has thus, in addition to drawing the peoples together into a physical community where distance has shrunk to a fraction of its former significance, made them more dependent upon each other's material resources if they would reap the advantages of invention. National restrictions stopping interchange not only impede further progress but threaten to drive us back to older techniques which, in many countries, could not support present populations at anything approaching their present standards of living.[7]

Yet Staley does not foresee or advocate the abandonment of national planning. The fault has not been in the attempt to organize economic activity for social ends, but in the shortsightedly nationalistic objectives and methods adopted. "As the demand for planning advances ahead of international government capable of planning, world economy finds itself being lopped off to fit the procrustean bed of nationalism."[8] Staley, like Condliffe, wishes to preserve a wide area of individual enterprise and competition. "The world economy of today and tomorrow must include means of making free enterprise and public planning work harmoniously side by side in the same country and means of carrying on exchange between countries whose economic systems are organized on different principles."[9] The problem is thus twofold—national and international. In the national sphere he suggests a rough delimitation of realms in which planning and competition should respectively prevail. The field of money management is one which he regards as suitable for all-over planning, while on the other hand competition centering around price and quality

[7] *Cf.* the van Zeeland Report, *loc. cit.*, p. 84.
[8] Eugene Staley, *World Economy in Transition*, New York, 1939, p. 165.
[9] *Ibid.*, p. 179.

should dominate the "marketing sector."[10] In all fields, however, the motive of planning must be positive, encouraging development, rather than negatively restrictive. The object, in other words, must be not to prevent national adjustments to developments abroad, but to foresee and facilitate such adjustments.[11]

Both in the book just cited and again in his paper on "The Economic Organization of Peace,"[12] Professor Staley sketches procedures and agencies for what he considers the necessary supranational co-ordination of economic policies. He recommends an organization made up of governmental representatives and delegates of economic groups such as consumers, workers, etc., with a small governing body and a permanent secretariat, and with the power of direct legislation in some matters (notably the supervision of international commodity control agencies) and of drafting treaties for subsequent state ratification in others. One function of this organization would be the preparation and direction of development programs which would benefit both the areas where development is most needed and the countries with heavy industries which, on the cessation of hostilities, will face unemployment. Another would be the harmonization of monetary policies through a world central bank, and the stimulation and direction of new investment. Exchange of information on business trends, and the guidance of national policies in such a way as to secure the best adaptation of national production to these trends, would be an important service to be rendered by the joint economic authority. Finally, this institution would be able to plan the migration and resettlement of populations within the limits where migration is socially desirable and economically profitable. Closely associated with the agencies already described would be an international colonial authority which would take over and administer colonial territories to be pooled by their present owners. Thus the

[10] *Ibid.*, pp. 180-187.
[11] *Ibid.*, p. 198.
[12] *International Conciliation*, No. 369, Carnegie Endowment for International Peace, April 1941.

areas most in need of economic as well as political development and suitable at the same time for new settlement would be taken out of the arena of interstate competition and administered on the open-door principle for their own and the general good.

Turning now to Meade and Hitch, *Economic Analysis and Policy* (New York, Oxford University Press, 1938), we find the same desiderata of international co-operation recognized. The book advocates agreements between states: 1) To provide employment by internal monetary policies. The governors of central banks would meet from time to time at the Bank of International Settlements to discuss the lowering or raising of interest rates simultaneously in all countries. Production would thus be stimulated or checked with due consideration of the international factors involved. 2) To minimize the fluctuations in exchange rates, the price of gold in each currency being fixed periodically by similar meetings at the Bank of International Settlements. The B. I. S. would check the disturbing movements of short-term capital by operating an international stabilization fund.[13] 3) To reduce barriers to international trade. Tariffs would be permitted only to protect infant industries or to prevent the terms of trade moving against a particular country. 4) To allow the free movement of capital across boundaries. 5) To reduce restrictions on migration, though not for the benefit of countries where no control is exercised over the increase of population.

In 1940 Mr. Meade returns to the attack with his *Economic Bases of a Durable Peace*. By this time his international agreements have ripened into agencies responsible to an International Authority. The Bank of International Settlements becomes an international central bank regulating the issue of international currency and having supreme control over exchange rates. The International Authority is to supervise the bodies already controlling

[13] Here, as in many other instances, the needs recognized by Staley and by Meade are identical with those stated in the van Zeeland Report, and the steps taken to meet them are, though less conservative, very similar. See particularly the Report, *loc. cit.*, pp. 87-99.

the production, distribution and prices of primary commodities, whether they be official agencies or private cartels. It will have power to prohibit exchange controls and clearing agreements and to secure the free cross-boundary flow of loans and investments. It will enforce the open door in colonial territories, perhaps by taking over the colonies from present holders and providing directly for their administration.

Among eminent economists who recognize the necessity of broad international planning, though they do not believe anything in the nature of a world-state possible in the near future, we may cite Dr. Moritz Bonn. His paper in the Annals of the American Academy of Political and Social Science for July 1941, advocates regional federations— Latin, Balkan, Northern, and Central European groups in Europe, and similar groups in the Far East and in South America. We are not precisely told what is to be the allover organization linking these groups together and responsible for the general economic planning which the author contemplates. He does, however, call for the co-operation of the principal Powers in the industrial development of China, tropical Africa, and Latin America. The colonies of tropical Africa are to be federated and presided over by a council including representatives of noncolonial Powers. At intervals throughout his paper, Dr. Bonn states his approval of such an association of "free and equal states and peoples" as was attempted in the League of Nations; and it may well be that the general setting in which he would place the specific arrangements which he describes is of the League type.

Institutions of economic co-operation are now regarded by many even of the most orthodox economists as an essential condition of peace and welfare. That they can only operate successfully as part of a general organization capable of preventing major political disturbances, is generally conceded. The problem is one and indivisible, though it has different aspects each requiring its own technical apparatus of solution. We are probably still very far, as Condliffe and Bonn believe, from the world-state which some publicists declare to be the only alternative to anarchy. But the universal organization without which international economic institutions can be but partial and temporary alleviations, and without which regional associations threaten to become wider bases of destructive competition and conflict, must have some of the elements of a world-state. Within the limits which surviving nationalisms will assuredly assign to it, it must operate as a world-government. The difference is less one of kind than of degree. To avoid the rather precise implications of "state" and yet to express the essential idea of an organized community, I have suggested the term "World Commonwealth."

The establishment of such a Commonwealth presupposes the defeat of Nazi Germany with its plan of master-races dominating vast imperia in Europe, Africa and Asia. Its immediate structure will depend upon the will of the United States, the British Nations and, it may now be hoped, of Soviet Russia. No sober estimate of the chances supports the expectation that the present chaos will be replaced by a complete and perfect world-government. There are still many persons in important positions, economists among others, who foresee nothing better than the most limited working arrangements among the principal Powers mapping out spheres of economic influence and upholding an armed peace. The grim prospect of repeated war which this "realistic" analysis holds out may well be rejected by the peoples. We should not, however, assume more than the most obviously necessary concessions of national "sovereignty" to supranational community. As time goes on, political and economic security alike will demand the expansion of this minimum and its evolution into a far-reaching and effective world-government. But there is little reason for believing that an interim period of gradual pacification, of trial and error, of education in world citizenship, can be avoided.

On the basis of the inter-war experience and of studies made by competent economists, it is already possible to sketch the minimum supranational institutions which the Powers upon whom will fall the responsibility for post-war settlement should seek to establish. The special groupings which now exist, or which may be formed after the war on the basis of regional contiguity or some other community of interest, may be counted upon to construct their own agencies of economic co-operation and control. We have already the example of the Inter-American Economic and Financial Advisory Committee and Development Commission, together with a draft convention for an Inter-American Bank. They can do useful service in exploring and developing regional resources, in adjusting labor supply to different local requirements, and in securing capital for desirable enterprise. But if their purpose is to restrict trade with the rest of the world, they are likely to do more harm than good. If the analysis in the earlier part of this chapter is at all valid, economic problems are those in which the universal approach is most imperative. It will be highly important, then, that any European, Far Eastern or Pan American economic machinery should be geared into a universal organization. Without such over-all co-ordination, the regional groups might become merely larger bases of attempted autarchy.

The following, therefore, is a tentative picture of the economic side of the World Commonwealth. The institutions described will not, it is believed, monopolize the area of economic activity, but will leave adequate scope still for private enterprise. They can, it is further believed, serve as instruments of co-operation between nations maintaining varying degrees of economic control.

At the last ordinary meeting of the Assembly, in 1939, the League of Nations adopted a report prepared under the direction of Mr. Stanley Bruce, delegate of Australia. This document, recognizing the importance of the economic and social work of the League, provided for its separation from political activities by taking it out of the Council's control and assigning it to an autonomous organization. States not belonging to the League would be invited to full participation, as in the International Labor Organization, and the directing body was to be made up of twenty-four state representatives and eight non-governmental members. The Assembly appointed an organizing committee under Hendrik Colijn, former Prime Minister of the Netherlands, which held its first meeting in February 1940 at The Hague. Needless to say, the whole project was soon suspended by events.

This move on the part of the League may be taken as a cue for post-war action. It lends support to Professor Staley's suggestion of an economic council made up partly of government delegates and partly of representatives chosen by economic groups. The Bruce Report contemplated a measure of autonomy for the new economic and social organization equivalent to that given to the International Labor Organization by Part XIII of the Treaty of Versailles. The principal constitutional relation was the I.L.O.'s dependence on the League for its budget. It soon transpired, however, that permanent liaison was necessary between the I.L.O. and various organs of the League; and it would be well to start the post-war economic and social agencies off with such a general responsibility to the Assembly of the World Commonwealth as will ensure the complete coordination of all activities seeking overlapping objectives.

Social activities should hardly come under the same immediate direction as those of an economic nature. One large part of the social work of the World Commonwealth will be identical with that carried out by the International Labor Organization in the inter-war period, and there will be strong support for continuing that institution along its present lines. It should be finally responsible, like the Economic and Financial Organization, to the Assembly of the World Commonwealth; and such social activities as the control of drug and white-slave traffics, public health and education, should be under similar distinct, though closely associated, control.

The Economic and Financial Organization will consist of the specific agencies mentioned below, all responsible to a Governing Body composed, like that of the International Labor Organization, partly of government delegates and partly of persons representing associated employers and workers. The Governing Body will in turn be responsible to the Assembly of the World Commonwealth. What follows is a minimum of essential institutions; more may be added as time goes on:

(1) A Trade Commission, instructed to secure the removal of quotas and other direct restrictions on trade and the reduction of tariffs. No further direct restrictions should be imposed, and no customs duties raised, without the consent of this body. It should also be given control of the activities of the international cartels which regulate the production and marketing of commodities like rubber, tin, copper, steel and oil. The fault commonly found with these associations is that they consider only the producer interest; and a proposal accepted by some economists, though scouted by others as futile, is that governmental and consumer representation on their directing boards should be made compulsory. Whether by this device or another, the cartels, which have proved their efficiency as instruments of international collaboration, should be taken into the supra-national organization and used in the general interest.

(2) A Central Bank, developed out of the present Bank of International Settlements, having authority to fix and funds to maintain exchange rates. No state would be free to establish exchange control without the consent of this Central Bank, which should have authority to define the purposes for which national control might be imposed and to terminate a permitted control when those purposes have been achieved.

(3) A Development Commission, having at its disposal substantial funds for financing public works and industrial installation with the double object of raising standards of living in undeveloped areas and furnishing new outlets for the productive capacity of existing industrial countries. International investments might be made to pass through this Commission for supervision of the purpose, terms, and se-

curity; and states might be forbidden to prevent or encourage cross-boundary capital movements save with its consent.

(4) A Migration and Settlement Commission, to deal with temporary problems like that of the present flux of refugees and with the general movement of populations in accordance with economic and social expediency. Some would place this in the Social Organization of the World Commonwealth, and certainly close collaboration with that organization will be necessary. Apart from pogroms and purges, however, the demand for freedom of migration is based primarily upon economic considerations and should in all cases be subject to expert and impartial economic scrutiny. On the whole, therefore, the very necessary supranational regulation of population movements and resettlement should be assigned to the Economic and Financial Organization, where it will also benefit by close co-ordination with development schemes.

The Economic and Financial Organization will of course have much to do with the administration, development, and settlement of present colonial areas. The general government of these territories is, however, assigned to another agency of the World Commonwealth. That agency, like most others, must work in constant consultation with the Economic and Financial Organization.

Nothing in the whole of this establishment will be more important for its success than the corps of administrative, research and secretarial personnel which must form its central and permanent working force. This will correspond to the Economic and Financial Section of the League of Nations Secretariat; but the increased scope and authority of the World Commonwealth in the economic sphere will mean both a larger and a different kind of staff.

Thus, the control of national restrictions on trade will require an expert inspectorate to operate in any country at need. The Economic and Financial Organization must not be content to sit at headquarters and receive reports from national officials. Similarly, the execution of development programs will involve setting up local offices of supervision. Problems of labor supply and migration will call for fieldworkers. The Organization should have representatives in the principal cartels and other instrumentalities of commodity control. The combination of knowledge, drive and tact which these tasks will demand, to say nothing of that complete internationalism of outlook which should characterize the members of a world civil service, will necessitate special measures, including probably an International Staff College, for the provision of qualified personnel.

CHAPTER XII

SUPRANATIONAL POLICE

The point at which the sharpest conflict appears between the traditional notion of the state and the needs of supranational organization is the proposal of a police power endowed with authority and strength to control the conduct of national governments. Immediately connected with the idea of police is the idea of coercion, and this is the direct negation of that illusory independence which is at once the joy of governments and the boast of excited mobs.

Belief in the necessity of independence for the state has been so successfully instilled into the citizen, and is so absolute, that he does not apply to state conduct the code of morals which stands behind the national law and forms the standard for his own acts and those of his fellow-citizens. Indeed, he has for centuries been consciously taught to reject such a code for his country. He does not therefore readily perceive the justification for measures of force applied to his state, though he accepts calmly the lawful restraint of the individual.

There has moreover been an oversight in most recent propaganda for peace. Some success has been achieved in fixing a moral stigma on war. But any application of force to a state, if resisted, becomes war in the popular and accepted sense. Constantly when there is talk of sanctions against states violating their obligations, the objection is raised—"But that means war"; and an immediate moral confusion presents itself because here, as elsewhere, the stigma accompanies the idea.

It is unfair to saddle the proposal of coercive action against countries guilty of aggression with the odium which quite properly attaches to war arbitrarily initiated by one state and employed as an "instrument of national policy." A clear distinction can and should be maintained by emphasis on the notion of the superstate community with a law having primacy over that of any state-member. That law observes precisely the same moral standards as the law of the state and, like the law of the state, must have force at its disposal to guarantee its application.

The immorality of war is, however, a consideration which influences relatively few, though they are among the more vocal, of the people whose thoughts and feelings constitute what is known as public opinion. The movement for a supranational police force, preached by Lord Davies in *The Problem of the Twentieth Century* and devoutly furthered by the New Commonwealth Institute of London, has encountered a more formidable obstacle in a combination of two fears. One is the fear that "our boys" will be sent fighting in remote corners of the earth; the other that the object of coercion will retaliate by such unpleasantly direct methods as dropping bombs on the cities which furnish the men and arms employed against him.

The detailed arrangements made for the establishment of supranational police in current plans go some way toward removing the grounds for these fears. They advocate a permanent professional force under an internationally constituted general staff responsible to the authorities of the supranational community. They pool existing navies under the same type of command. At the same time they deprive individual states of heavy artillery and tanks, warships and military aircraft. The calm acceptance of the use of naval forces in remote waters is some indication that the distaste for distant punitive expeditions is one that attaches to "citizen armies" rather than regular professional services whose personnel choose their profession without geographical reservations. The disarmament which is always part of the plans deprives the aggressor country of the means of effective retaliation, while the fact that the coercive action is decreed by the supranational community and carried out by its own forces relieves the member states of individual responsibility.

It is impossible, however, to eliminate all danger of destructive retaliation. An aggressor country which, in spite of all precautions, has acquired sufficient military power to set out on the path of violence may well select conveniently situated neighbors for its revenge. Brigands within the state have from time to time achieved such a position and adopted such tactics. They have not thereby persuaded the body of citizens that the national organization and its police are a danger rather than a protection.

The police analogy is rejected by some serious writers on the ground that the proportion of power in any supranational community as against the individual state is much less than that residing in the state as against the individual citizen. This argument would have arrested the whole process whereby the clan or tribe has been subordinated to the city-state, the city-state to the nation-state, the state to the federation in many lands. The problem is essentially one of proportion of means to ends; but its solution is greatly aided by the larger unit's assumption of authority and protection extending not simply to the subordinated groups, but to the individual members of the groups, with an accompanying division of the citizen's loyalty. The resident of Massachusetts looks for a large part of his security, and is subject in a large part of his conduct, to the government, not of Massachusetts, but of the United States. His status as an American citizen is at least as precious to him as his membership in the Commonwealth of Massachusetts. Thus it comes about that the act of an official of a subordinate group in violation of the law of the larger community is not necessarily regarded as a group-act or supported as such by the group.

Of course the supremacy of the central authority in its proper sphere, though immediately provided in a constitution, may require time for its establishment in fact. In the United States the process involved a long series of interpretative judgments by the Supreme Court and was only complete after a civil war. It remains true, however, that the course of political development has been the integration of small communities into larger units and that the present demands of security and prosperity point urgently to active facilitation of this trend. There is no difference in kind between that centralization of power which produced the modern state and the contemporary effort for supranational organization. The latter is merely the beginning of a new stage in a continuous process, and the needs which dictate this further development are of like nature with those that inspired each of the advances already accomplished.

Far from being a false analogy from the growth of the modern state, then, the tentative approach to the creation of supranational police is the same process in a larger sphere.

Nearly all the current plans of organized peace concur on the need for a police force under supranational authority powerful enough to operate successfully against states resisting the common will. But they differ considerably in their treatment of the matter. Some of them drop it after declaring the principle. Others, because they are concerned only with the European scene, give the specifications in more or less detail for a Continental force without considering the impact of extra-European interests on its operation. Still others make all sanctions a regional affair and link the various regional associations in a purely co-operative League divested of any compulsory power. Finally some of our writers add to their arrangements for regional police a more or less powerful protective and disciplinary establishment of world-wide scope and responsible ultimately to a single world authority. Thus Buell in his *Isolated America*, having linked up his regional associations in a world society of nations under a World Council, gives that Council command over a "symbolic and preventive" police force which would be available in addition to the regional forces to check nascent aggression or occupy territory in dispute.

As an eventual goal, the creation of a unified world force with military, naval and air arms is beyond criticism; and to do them justice that is the way in which it is regarded by those of our writers who endorse the proposal. If even the democratic world is still far from willing to federate in one union, still less likely is it that the world as a whole can be brought in any near future under one authority exercising the dominant military power which is an essential feature of such union. If there were any immediate prospect of achieving this, it would be needless to labor the preliminary steps of regional federation; we could proceed at once to work out the detail of a federal union for the world.

Men who work for progress must choose for themselves whether they shall eschew all compromise and direct their energies to the immediate realization of the complete ideal, or concentrate on a less perfect but more attainable objective from which they can make a fresh start toward the ideal. In the first case they risk a neutralizing classification as fanatics; in the second they risk condemnation for tolerance and inadequacy. In this study I take the latter course, fearing lest in attempting all we gain nothing.

Those plans which advocate a supreme force under one joint authority in Europe are already ambitious enough. This in effect means a single federal union of Europe, for I repeat that submission to one dominant military and police authority is the chief hurdle in federalization. More probably the next forward step in the political development of that continent is the grouping of its various nations in several parallel federations. That a trend in this direction already existed before the present war, in Scandinavia, among the Baltic States, in the Basin of the Danube and in the Balkans, is proved not merely by intellectual speculation but by political discussion. As this is being written the Czech and Polish governments in exile are discussing postwar federation of their two countries. Of these groupings the Western federation, which must eventually include Germany, will be the most advanced industrially, socially and culturally, and the most powerful. It will be the controlling factor in European politics, acting, it is to be hoped, through an association in which all the federal unions, including Soviet Russia, will participate. Some considerable time will elapse before this association is given command of a force sufficient to impose its will. In that interval discipline is likely to be in the hands of the pooled forces of the Western federation, which will secure the progressive disarmament of its own individual members and of the other European unions. Admittedly one of the delicate problems in this program will be the collaboration of the Soviet Union, over which the tutelage still possible for other groups will not be feasible. Yet, with the conduct of the Soviets in the Geneva League as an indication, there is ground for hope that the problem will be solved, even though we may be less optimistic than Mr. Jennings in his *A Federation for Western Europe* about the eventual triumph of democracy in Russia and the possibility of bringing the Soviet Union into the Western Federation.

Along with this development in Europe it is not unreasonably optimistic to expect an increasing integration of the Pan American community. Considerable strides in this direction have been made in recent years, particularly since the meeting of the Montevideo Conference in 1933. The ratification and coming into force of the very comprehensive system for the peaceful settlement of disputes drawn up at Washington in 1929, the agreements at Buenos Aires and Lima in 1936 and 1938 to maintain a common policy of neutrality, and the action taken under those agreements at successive meetings of the foreign ministers since the outbreak of war in September 1939, the joint pressure brought to bear to end the conflict between Bolivia and Paraguay, and the current effort of Washington to co-ordinate the defense of the hemisphere against political, economic and military penetration from outside—all of these are indications that the need of organization is increasingly realized.

There has never yet been any actual approach to the establishment of a common force to prevent aggressions between nations of the hemisphere or to protect them against external aggression, though this was one object of the Congress of Panama in 1826. Responsibility for defense was long ago assumed by the United States, and certain police functions have from time to time been performed by the same country under unwelcome riders to the Monroe Doctrine. The contemporary threat of German invasion may lead to the creation of a joint force, if only to forestall unilateral action by the United States which, dictated by necessity, would hardly respect the jealously asserted sovereignty of the Latin American states. One of the functions of such a force, in addition to resisting invasion, would be to put down Fascist-Nazi risings leading to European domination. The force once established to meet an emergency would not necessarily disband with the passing of that danger.

At Ogdensburg in August 1940, the President of the United States and the Prime Minister of Canada made an agreement which may lead far in the direction just indicated. A Joint Defense Board has been created to co-ordinate measures of continental defense. From that to a joint force is not a great step, nor does it seem likely that the expediency of extending the agreement beyond the United States and Canada can long be denied.

At the best, however, any arrangement of this nature in the Western hemisphere will, for some time to come, be of a contractual rather than constitutional character. It is hardly likely that any joint force would achieve the position of a federal army. It would consist rather of temporary contingents under international command regulated by treaty, and would be liable to all the defects of the Continental Army under the first American Constitution. It would closely resemble the army that might have been assembled by the League of Nations if it had ever embarked on military sanctions.

For peace in the Pacific, the proposal now most supported is that the Nine Power Treaty should be restored to life, this time with the addition of the Soviet Union among its signatories and with provision for joint action against a party violating its clauses. Here also would be a system, not of a federal nature but approaching the League type, having recourse in circumstances defined by the treaty to contributory police measures. The arrangement would be subject to all the weaknesses revealed in the sanctions machinery of the League Covenant; but it would be workable (as the

League would have been) given the will. It may be held that the proviso of determined purpose begs the whole question of the merit of such a pact; but the value of a program of action is surely self-evident. If the Nine Power Treaty of 1921 had contained, instead of the vague obligation to communicate and consult, a clause binding the United States and Great Britain to join in defined measures of enforcement, it is at least arguable that the ruin of the organization for peace in the Pacific, and the closely connected ruin of the League, would have been averted. We may take the lesson of experience without crying over spilt milk.

Developments of the sort just described are less perfect, but more probable, than any scheme of uniform regional federations embracing the whole world. We shall therefore be prudent in planning for the co-operation of dissimilar associations of states—associations conforming to different conditions of geography, political evolution, cultural tradition and social habit. It may be that events have brought us to the eve of superstate organization in Europe, with the accompanying creation of unified forces for purposes of internal order and external defense; but there is little evidence of any tendency as yet to the division of the oceans into naval zones policed by two navies absorbing and replacing national fleets and carefully balanced in strength. This part of the plan which we described in a previous chapter as that of an English group is too remote to be included in any program of immediate post-war organization. The strategic distribution of the British and American navies in the Atlantic and Pacific respectively, whether that be the result of agreement or an entirely spontaneous response to separate estimates of the national interest, is still a far cry from the contributory creation of non-national naval forces operating under supranational authority.

This conclusion has been disputed on the ground that the present war is slowly but surely bringing about a union of American and British forces. The union will have to be maintained at least long enough to set a new supranational organization securely on its feet, and during that time British and American arms will in fact be acting as world police. Why should they not combine in that capacity either by mere bilateral agreement or as the military, naval and air establishment of the world commonwealth? My answer is that even if the American and British peoples were willing indefinitely to supply and be taxed for these forces (which is at least questionable) the other nations would not indefinitely submit to British-American coercion. A world police would have to be thoroughly internationalized, and this involves universal federation.

I have spoken of the police power and the functioning of supranational military, naval and air forces as one and the same thing, while admitting that defense against attack from outside would be one function of such forces. I regard the whole business of keeping the peace within a federation and enforcing the obligations of federated states *inter se* as one of police, even though this may involve methods commonly described as military. The crux of the problem of federalization is submission to action of this nature directed by a central authority, whereas the union of forces under one command against a common enemy is already a familiar feature of temporary alliances. The latter function of the common force is, moreover, destined to diminish with the strengthening organization of the world-community. In the ultimate objective it completely disappears, the task of order and security as between the various associations of states being taken over by one universal police force unified and distributed in some such way as that sketched by the English group mentioned above. The distinction between the police and the armed forces, between civil and military functions, is one belonging to the stage of international anarchy, and there is therefore some point as we approach world government in emphasizing the civil character of all agencies of compulsion.

To sum up, I believe that while certain parts of Europe may be ripe for willing submission to federalized police establishments guaranteeing the fulfillment of articles of association, and while agreements on contributory joint enforcement of sanctions on League lines may be possible in other areas, the exercise of police power is not likely to be more than regional in scope for some time to come. This amounts to saying that any common organization supplementing the various regional associations sketched by our writers will not for the present be backed by any other military force than that which states or regional associations may from time to time be willing to put at its disposal. My reason for this conclusion is that I do not see evidence yet of a sufficiently widespread and powerful sense of the community of the human race to serve as a basis for what would amount to a world-federation. Failing that evidence, while one may ardently desire to foster and spread this sense, one cannot adopt a project of world-police as part of what sets out to be an immediate program of progress in international politics.

CHAPTER XIII

SUPRANATIONAL COURTS

There is something approaching unanimous agreement that the judicial establishment which forms part of every project of international organization should have compulsory jurisdiction. That the state should have the arbitrary power to decide whether or not it will submit to judicial examination of its claims is more and more widely regarded as an untenable feature of the sovereignty doctrine. It is of the essence of community that the boundaries of individual right should be determined by impartial authority rather than by the respective strength of the claimants.

A dangerous qualification is, however, usually attached to the principle of compulsory jurisdiction. Most writers limit it to what they call "justiciable" or "legal" disputes, without saying who is to decide whether a dispute falls within this category. If this discretion is left to the parties, the rule of compulsory jurisdiction becomes illusory; for every claim in which the state feels a strong interest will be described as "nonjusticiable" or "political" rather than legal. The result is the same as if the old-fashioned exception, withdrawing matters of vital interest or affecting the national honor from the operation of arbitration treaties, were retained in so many words.

It is worth realizing that all disputes are, in one important sense, legal or justiciable. The claim of any disputant is either supported by the law as it stands, or it is not; and that itself is a legal question to be answered by a court. If Japan claims commercial advantages in China, and China denies them, there is a legal dispute which can be settled by a court in the sense that a court will always be able to give judgment saying whether the claim is supported by existing legal right. If it is not, Japan loses its case.

Such a judgment, however, may be anything but the end

of the matter. Japan may go on pressing her claim on the ground that the law is inequitable and subjects her to unreasonable hardship. Analogous situations are constantly presenting themselves in the internal life of nations. The whole history of labor legislation is full of examples. Employers have rights and the courts uphold them against the claims of employees. Often a judge remarks that the law is inhuman but that he must apply it, for it is not his function but that of the legislature to change the law. Workmen have been able to persuade the legislatures that the existing law was inequitable and in a hundred ways it has been changed.

In this sense, and in this alone, the expression "non-justiciable dispute" is warranted. The claim raised by a state may be of a sort which merits a change in the existing law. The resulting dispute cannot be substantially settled and disposed of merely by a judgment stating what the law is. The great difficulty in dealing with such cases has been that there has been no defined legislative authority in the international sphere to which they could be referred for consideration and, where the need is proved, action.

But the fact that such claims may occur does not justify a state in withholding a dispute from judicial examination. The state's own assertion that its claim is of such a type cannot be accepted as final. There may be cases where the inequity of the situation is obvious, and where therefore immediate application to a legislative authority will save time and possibly bloodshed. Frequently, however, there will be room for doubt, and the judicial process will be the best way of determining whether any *prima facie* justification for an amendment of the law exists.

In yet another class of dispute, what is needed for settlement is not a change in the general rule or law but an equitable interpretation taking into account peculiar features of the specific case. Many rules of law leave a measure of discretion to the judge, and qualification of the general principle to avoid unbearable hardship in a particular situation is a familiar function of courts everywhere.

For both reasons, (a) because the question of the adequacy of the existing law may be best answered by the court, and (b) because an equitable interpretation of the sort that judges are trained and accustomed to make may meet the need, care should be taken not to exclude all jurisdiction of the courts even in so-called "nonjusticiable" or "political" disputes.

The movement for an international equity tribunal, as sponsored for example by the New Commonwealth Society from its headquarters in London, goes so far as to entrust to a judicial body the function of changing the law of nations. This has sometimes been done by two states through instructions, addressed to the tribunal set up to deal with a dispute, to decide *ex aequo et bono*. Decision *ex aequo et bono* is something different from the equitable interpretation referred to above. It means that the judges, finding no established law which meets the needs of the situation submitted to them, make a rule for it according to their ideas of what is just and right in the circumstances. The Permanent Court of International Justice was authorized to do this in Article 38 of its Statute, but only with the consent of the parties. What is usually involved looks like an addition to the law rather than a variation from existing rules, though there is nothing to prevent this also being agreed to. But in any event the decision makes law only for the parties and only for the particular case.

In the absence of any supranational legislature, the use of judges to produce changes in the law as changing circumstances demand has much to commend it. To a greater extent than is ever acknowledged, new law is made by the judges in all states without any special authorization. In two of the most famous arbitrations in modern history, The Behring Sea Fur Seals Case and the North Atlantic Fisheries Case, Great Britain and the United States requested the arbiters to draw up new rules for the regulation of fisheries and subsequently adopted these in their national legislation. Long legal training and judicial experience are a good preparation for weighing arguments and evidence even in unfamiliar matter, and the amendments in the legal system which judges may be led to make are unlikely to be hasty or ill-considered. Democratic theory, however, demands for purposes of legislation a broader representation of the various elements in society than is likely to be found in a judicial body. For filling in the many interstices of the law made by custom or by parliament judges are indispensable, but no modern community will assign the heavy and constant task of legislation to bodies primarily designed to say what the law is rather than to create it.

The problem of peaceful change, therefore, can be only partially solved by courts, even with the attribution to decide *ex aequo et bono*.

The conditions, scope and nature of their authority are not the only questions relating to international courts which need reconsideration if and when the opportunity comes to re-establish and strengthen the organization for peace. The Permanent Court of International Justice rendered great service both in the settlement of actual disputes and in the further development of the law of nations. But it was never free of the suspicion of political influence by the powerful states of the period. Few courts, if any, are entirely free of such suspicion; but the Permanent Court suffered under a greater weight of it than most. The fact that with one or two minor exceptions its judges voted in accordance with the claims of the states from which they came is always cited against it.

Affection presses upon judgment in the most subtle ways, and it is not necessary to seek dishonesty or corruption to explain the identity of a man's opinions with the case put forward by his country. But in the establishment or re-establishment of any court designed to apply a supranational law, certain obvious precautions ought to be taken to reduce the likelihood of undue national influence.

In no case should the court dealing with a claim between two states include nationals of either. Article 31 in the Statute of the Permanent Court, which provided for the special representation of a state not normally having a national on the Court, in litigation where the state was a party, was a violation of the essential character of judicial tribunals. The Article should have called instead for the withdrawal of any judge whose state is involved in the proceedings. Everything which encourages the notion of representation in the composition of the Court must be avoided. There is indeed much to be said for the denationalization of all permanent international judges.

The termination of national representation on the Court has been opposed by some of those most closely concerned in its work. Their contention is that the popular conviction of the justness of a decision is as important as the fact of justness. People, it is argued, will have more confidence if they have a countryman on the Bench. But can the fact of having a judge in the Court, whose vote was overruled by his fellow-judges, really carry conviction of justice to the people of the losing state? Surely the connection between justice and impartiality is one understood even by the masses, and the exclusion of national judges in cases involving their states is an obvious safeguard of impartiality.

The further argument, that the national judge brings to the Court an intimate and trustworthy knowledge of the local law and conditions bearing on the litigation, seems equally inconclusive. As in state courts, the Bench can obtain such knowledge from counsel and expert witnesses, if not from its own researches.

The judges should have life-tenure up to maximum age of seventy or possibly seventy-five years and subject to dismissal for misconduct or inefficiency, the authority of dismissal resting with the body which appoints them. To limit the judge to a term of nine years, after which, if not reelected, he must hope to find a continuation of his career in his own country, means subjecting him to strong temptation to retain the favor of his national authorities.

Some of the advocates of European federation, apparently in order to avoid the multiplication of new institutions, would employ the Permanent Court of International Justice for the settlement of disputes between the federated states. From the beginning, however, the federation would inevitably raise numerous legal questions. One of its essential virtues is that it would provide a ready forum for many grievances that now remain unsettled or lead to violence, while one of its inevitable vices is that the division of powers between state and federal authorities requires constant judicial definition. There would be more than a little risk of fixing permanently on the World Court the stigma that it is a purely European affair.

The United States of Europe, however small the nucleus with which the federation begins, will need its own federal judicial organ. The Permanent Court of International Justice must be retained for the adjudication of disputes involving members of different federations or regional associations. Its jurisdiction in this wider sphere should be made compulsory and universal at the earliest possible moment, even though the world organization to enforce submission to it and compliance with its judgments be lacking. Such organization has never yet been established, but undertakings to submit to adjudication and to accept the decision arrived at have abundantly proved their utility. It is hardly to be denied, for example, that the long reign of peace between the United States and Great Britain was made possible only by arrangements for arbitration; and the student of Anglo-American and Canadian-American relations has before him cogent evidence that the danger of serious conflict is greatly reduced by the establishment, in advance of any quarrel, of institutions to deal with possible disputes. That the United States has appreciated the value of general treaties of arbitration, and of standing bodies of arbiters, is shown by the network of such arrangements to which it is a party.

A court has compulsory jurisdiction when the members of the community which it serves are bound to come before it on being summoned. The recipient of summons has no liberty to refuse to appear even if the matter in which he is called to answer appears on the face of it to fall outside those for which the court is declared competent in the instrument creating it. One normal function of courts is that of deciding whether or not they have jurisdiction in the cases brought before them. In recent treaties of arbitration there is usually only one important limitation—the restriction to "legal" or "justiciable" disputes already mentioned; and we have argued that the court itself is the proper body to decide any question arising under this classification.

Some opposition still exists to attributing to supranational courts these normal powers of state tribunals, and though theorists are agreed upon the need for compulsory jurisdiction some of them doubt the readiness of the peoples to bow to this need. An examination of the record of the Permanent Court of International Justice gives hope that this obstacle will not prove so formidable as is sometimes supposed. More than forty states had at one time accepted the obligation to submit to the Court their disputes with other states accepting the same obligation. Usually the obligation was limited to a five-year period, but some acceptances were for ten years and others had no time limit. Between 1921 and 1934, that is to say, there was a real approach toward universal recognition of a duty to submit to judicial settlement. This notable advance in so short a time justifies the belief that, given another opportunity, a humanity again war weary may go the whole way.

It may be noted that I have made no distinction between judicial process and arbitration. In the international field the difference is hardly more than one of name. The records of modern arbitration for a hundred years show that the most successful arbitral method has been almost as strictly judicial as the procedure of national courts. The decisions that have left most bitterness and complaint have been those subject to the suspicion of political conciliation rather than adjudication.

Where a difference does exist it is between arbitration or adjudication on the one hand and conciliation on the other. Many treaties have provided for the submission of any type of dispute, whether "legal" or "political," to a Conciliation Commission for investigation and report with a view to adjustment. The object contemplated here is rather amiable compromise than judgment, the recommendations of the conciliators may override legal rights, and their findings are in any case not binding on the parties, who may accept and act upon them or reject them totally. Where settlement is not thus reached, some benefit may nevertheless have accrued in the cooling down of irritation through the lapse of time and the preparation of national tempers for submission to adjudication. Such was the rationale of the Bryan Treaties concluded by the United States with a number of other countries from 1913 on, of the first chapter of the elaborate General Act for the Pacific Settlement of Disputes drawn up by the League of Nations in 1928, and of the Conciliation Conventions in the Pan American system of peaceful settlement established at Washington in 1929.

A great deal of time and negotiation has gone into the conclusion of arrangements for conciliation. Very little use has ever been made of the result, while on the other hand the practice of reference to international adjudication proper has grown by leaps and bounds. One reason for the difference is probably that the function of conciliation is already pretty well provided for in the ordinary mechanism of diplomacy. I suggest, however, that the facts indicate greater confidence in the judicial method; and I infer that future effort to forestall recourse to violence in the assertion of national claims will be well advised to concentrate on creating courts or extending the jurisdiction of those which already exist.

In Mr. Ivor Jennings' federation, the judges of the Supreme Court are appointed by the Federal President after nomination by a Judiciary Commission. The Judiciary Commission is appointed by the States' House. This method seems excellent, except that the bicameral legislature is undesirable, for reasons advanced by Professor Scelle in the article summarized in our chapter on "Ascendancy of the Federal Idea." In any federation that may be established the appointment of the Commission should accordingly be entrusted to the single federal House.

The maintenance of the Permanent Court of International Justice is usually connected with the re-establishment of an amended League of Nations. If, as has been suggested by some critics, the Council of the League should be abolished—a view supported in our next chapter—then the election of judges should be assigned to the Assembly after nomination by a Judiciary Commission appointed by the same body.

CHAPTER XIV

SUPRANATIONAL LEGISLATION AND PEACEFUL CHANGE

We have seen that one of the reasons advanced for the recognition of war as a legal institution is the absence of a legislative body with universal authority which could make such amendments in existing law as are demanded by important changes in circumstances. The argument is that legalized violence is better from the point of view of expediency and even of morality than a petrified *status quo*. If war is to be ousted from its place as a regrettable but necessary method of desirable reform, we must find a substitute device for changing outworn institutions and situations that have become unfair.

It has also been admitted that while courts may be useful in this process, as agencies well qualified to say whether an amendment in the law is needed, they cannot be expected to fill anything like the role of the legislature in the modern state. Something in the nature of a supranational legislature is greatly needed. What are the chances, and how should we approach the problem?

In areas where new federations occur the need will be met, for all local purposes, by that development. Federal constitutions will as a matter of course provide for federal legislatures. If there is any debate, it will turn on the composition of these bodies. On this point it is to be hoped that attention will be paid to Professor Scelle's brief for unicameral legislatures in his article on "Le Problème du Fédéralisme" in *Politique Etrangère* for April 1940.

The best that can be said for the bicameral system is that it serves as a lure for small states, who are assured of a representation in the second chamber out of proportion to their population and their importance in world politics. Historically, second chambers have ceased to represent state interests and have rapidly divided on party lines similar to those in the Lower House. Thus the theoretical function of the Upper House to protect the autonomy of the states has in fact been abandoned to the federal court, which invalidates acts found to lie outside the constitutional limitations of the federal authority.

As for the other traditional function of Upper Houses—that of serving as a curb on rash legislation by Houses of Representatives—it has long been a moot question whether this is not an undesirable check, in the hands of vested minority interests, on reforms believed by the majority to be for the common good. The modern tendency is to restrict this negative power of Senates and State Houses by enabling Representative Assemblies to enact laws over their veto. This is a continuation of the trend which long ago abolished in a number of progressive democracies the right of the Upper House to veto or amend money bills.

Few constitutionalists would erect a States' House in any new federation for the performance of such duties in the ratification of treaties and in the appointment of officers of state as those attributed to the Senate in the Constitution of the United States. Some of these duties should be left to the body whose composition makes it a more accurate interpreter of the common will; others, such as the appointment of officers, are the proper function of the government subject only to the general supervision of the Representative Assembly.

For these reasons it would be a mistake to complicate the machinery of any forthcoming federation of states in Europe or elsewhere with bodies designed to give equal or weighted representation to the states as such. Most writers are agreed that everything must be done to ensure that divisions in the legislature should be along lines of opinion and policy rather than by state. It is an inconsistency to set up a body composed of representatives of states, and to count on time to fuse these delegates into parties. The national attachments and local interests of the members of a single, popular Assembly, reinforced by the constitutional guardianship of a Supreme Court, will afford adequate protection for the legitimate claims of individual states. Insofar as a combination of the representatives of small states in a States' House could outvote the greater states, this would permit a minority to prevent, for the sake of state sovereignty, developments sought by the majority of the people in the federation as a whole. It should not be forgotten that the purpose of federation is the welfare of human beings, not the further sanctification of that abstract entity the state. No attempt should be made to conceal the fact that in all matters handed over to the union the sovereignty of the individual states goes by the board.

As for the basis of representation, there is good support for the proposal that this should be proportional. If it is desired that the whole activity of the federation should be directed by the forces having the greatest numerical support among the total electorate, the best way to secure this is to make the government responsible to a popular assembly elected by a system of proportional representation. The constituencies would be the states themselves, and Mr. Ivor Jennings' suggestion, in *A Federation for Western Europe*, of one member per half-million electors would be a suitable measure for that area. The political groupings of members from the different states would tend to combine, and the largest of these combinations would dominate the federal assembly. The objection that this would mean the instability of government which has marked French politics is not self-evident, though worthy of careful consideration. The relatively limited field of federal competence should not produce the multiple division of parties that can result from proportional representation in internal politics. Alignments on matters of defense, foreign policy, external economic relations and colonial administration have in fact been comparatively simple. The very necessity of forming parties across old national lines should tend to broaden the dividing issues and so to limit the number of groupings.

The members of the federal legislature, not being appointed by the states but elected by the people by direct universal suffrage, do not represent the states as such, but the electors; and it is hoped that they will be grouped around policies rather than state interests. Nevertheless there is likely to be, especially at first, a marked tendency to state blocs, in which case the demands of the most numerous state may prevail over the interests of the federation as a whole. Imagine India or China in a federation with unqualified representation by population. Even if the union be a purely European one, the disparity between German members of the legislature and English or French members might well militate against the general interest. This is one of the arguments in favor of a second House in which the membership from the various states is, if not equal, more nearly so. But this cure errs in the opposite direction, since it enables the small states to exercise a negative influence out of all proportion to their combined populations. This difficulty is met in some projects, at least partially, by a provision enabling the People's House to enact laws, under certain conditions and by repeated vote, over the veto of the States' House. But in precisely the same measure the second House ceases to be a safeguard against national "swamping."

We are here at grips with one of the main obstacles to the federalization of communities with strongly developed nationalism. It may well be necessary at first, while accepting the principle of representation proportional to the size of the national electorate, to qualify it in such a way as to reduce the potential strength of grouped members from any single state. A superiority in number of deputies might be conceded to great populations which would not, however, be so great as to constitute a real threat. As the sentiment of federal community grows—and such growth would be at once a condition and a result of continued success—and parties develop across state lines, the true proportion can be established.

Federal unions of European states, with the creation of legislatures and executive agencies having authority over peoples whose conflicts have hitherto been the most prolific sources of war, would make for a more peaceful world. If universal federation were possible, then the enactment and execution of laws dealing with matters of common interest for the whole would be the business of a world legislature and government. The majority, perhaps, of theorists admit that this would be the perfect solution of the vast problems of world politics, though some fear a colorless uniformity that would leave no spice in life. The view taken in this book is that universal federalization will be a long process, and that to proceed more or less immediately after this war to set up such an organization—even if a strong group of nations imposed it—would mean glossing over disruptive differences of national outlook and method. It has also been argued in the chapter on "The British-American Front" that the best way to resume the task of supranational organization will be to supplement existing or potential regional groupings with a universal association bearing more resemblance to a league than to a federal union.

But if we have no world federation, hence no world parliament properly so called, how are we to meet the acknowledged need of peaceful change—the need, in other words, of amending the universal supranational law as fundamental conditions change, and of altering particular situations which, though legal, have become inequitable? It was pointed out in the chapter on "Law and the Community of States" that this function can be adequately performed only if we introduce decision by majority. How can we gain acceptance for the principle of majority decision, and how enforce majority decisions, without going far beyond the league type of association and into the sphere of federation?

It must be admitted at once that without world federation this problem can only be partially solved. But some steps leading in the right direction may be taken once the victory over Hitlerism is won.

In the first place, the general assembly of the universal association can be authorized in the instruments providing for its creation to make by majority vote decisions legally binding on all its members. This power will of course be limited to the matters specifically assigned to the universal association, and the majority rule will itself tend to restrict the range of business which states will be ready to hand over to this superstate organization. It will be more conducive to progress, however, to create a body of limited competence exercised by majority vote than one covering a multitude of matters which it can only touch on condition of unanimity. Nothing is less calculated to win for an institution the respect which its successful operation needs than the practice of pious resolutions to which no one is bound to give effect because in order to win unanimity they are worded so vaguely as to impose no obligation. True, a sanction over and above the mere legal obligation may be needed to secure performance; but it is at least a beginning to give the character of law to enactments supported by the greater part of the assembly. Even though this law-making effect should in some cases be made to depend upon a qualified majority, like three-quarters or two-thirds, progress would still be possible.

Majority decision is not totally unknown in international institutions, though hitherto it has been allowed to play only a very small role. We find it admitted in matters which governments are content to regard as "administrative." For example, proposals to modify the conventions or regulations of the Universal Postal Union become binding in certain carefully limited cases on a two-thirds or simple majority vote; and the regulations concerning certificates, licenses, log-books, etc., appended to the Air Navigation Convention of Paris, 1919, can be amended by a three-fourths vote of the International Commission for Air Navigation. In a more limited sphere, the European Commission of the Danube, whose business it is to secure free and improved navigation and equal treatment for all flags on that river, enacts its regulations and makes its other decisions by majority vote. Questions of mere procedure are commonly left to majority decision. In Article 5 of the Covenant of the League of Nations these are extended to include "the appointment of Committees to investigate particular matters."

Somewhat more important, since they affect matters of substance rather than procedure, are the admission of new members to the League by two-thirds of the Assembly (Art. 1), and the amendment of the Covenant by the "Members of the League whose Representatives compose the Council and by a majority of the Members of the League whose representatives compose the Assembly" (Art. 26). In the text last mentioned, however, sovereignty is safeguarded by the clause—"No such amendments shall bind any Member of the League which signifies its dissent therefrom, but in that case it shall cease to be a Member of the League."

Arbitral and judicial institutions, finally, have completely escaped the bane of unanimity. This is not surprising, since adjudication would hardly be possible at all if it were made to depend on complete agreement among the judges. It is for that reason that most treaties of arbitration provide either for decision by one impartial third party or for an umpire who has the casting vote when the arbiters representing the disputing states differ. In the Permanent Court of International Justice all questions are settled by a majority of the judges present. The real wrench to sovereignty occurs when a state agrees to submit to the decision of any authority which from the moment of that submission can operate without its further consent. Accordingly the state either refuses to submit at all or, since it regards an external decision as desirable, accepts a workable arrangement for arriving at such decision.

What is needed now is an extension of the principle of majority decision considerably beyond the circumscribed area in which it has hitherto been allowed to operate. Two types of occasion present themselves for its use. One is desirable clarification and amendment of the general law; the other, the adjustment of inequitable situations as between two or more states.

The need for clarification and amendment, and at the same time the difficulty of meeting this need under a system requiring unanimity both for binding declarations of existing law and for the addition of new rules, may be well illustrated from the history of the attempt made by the League of Nations to codify certain branches of international law. After some years of patient research, of discussion in a committee of experts, and of consultation to ascertain the views of governments, three subjects were proposed for codification at The Hague in 1930. These were the law of territorial waters, the law of nationality, and the law of responsibility for injuries to the persons or property of foreigners. When the conference was held, only some portions of the law of nationality reached the stage of draft agreements to be submitted to states for ratification. In every other part of the agenda it became apparent in the deliberations that anything approaching unanimity either as to what the law now is or as to what it should be was impossible, and the conference broke up in almost total failure. Yet in some of the most important questions under consideration a powerful majority, including the great states with the strongest material interest in the subject, would have accepted drafts laid before the conference or its committees.

Inequities as between two or more states, giving rise to disputes between them, were included in the broad terms of Article 15 of the Covenant of the League of Nations. The members undertook to submit to the Council any dispute likely to lead to a rupture, which had not been submitted to arbitration or judicial settlement; and the article makes a wary approach to the majority principle. The parties are bound not to go to war if the whole Council apart from themselves agrees upon terms of settlement. If a mere majority apart from themselves agrees, they are left free to act as they "shall consider necessary for the maintenance of right and justice." The same article provides that the Council may of its own motion, and must at the request of either party, refer the dispute to the Assembly. If the Assembly then adopts a report concurred in by the representatives of the members making up the Council and by a majority of the other members of the League, exclusive in each case of the representatives of the parties in dispute, the parties are bound not to resort to war. Article 15 was applied in the

Manchurian dispute at the request of China. The Assembly, to which the case was referred, adopted its report on February 24, 1933, with only one dissenting voice, that of Japan. It recommended the establishment of autonomous government in Manchuria, with recognition of continuing Chinese sovereignty, and direct negotiations for the withdrawal of Japanese troops. League members were recommended not to recognize the Japanese puppet state of Manchukuo. No sanction other than this non-recognition was suggested, and Japan, which very soon announced its withdrawal from the League, proceeded unchecked in its invasion of Chinese territory. The failure here was not one of the mechanics of decision but of the mechanics of enforcement. Supranationally organized economic power might well have been sufficient in this case, without the intervention of supranationally organized military power; but neither of them existed.

The leading members of the League were always reluctant to bring Article 15 into play, precisely because it meant decision against the will and vote of one of the parties. This involved the risk of weakening the organization by the withdrawal of the losing member, and this is what actually occurred when Japan and Italy were the culprits. Yet, if any efficient joint agency is to be created for the settlement of conflicts and preservation of peace, this issue must be squarely faced. The League procedure under Article 15 provided means whereby a single member-state might be prevented from legally resorting to war to enforce a claim against another. But if the wrongdoer could persuade another member of the Council to vote against his condemnation, he was left legally free to follow his own devices. Even this modest assumption of authority was studiously avoided except as a last resort. Every method of dealing with the dispute without offending even an obvious delinquent was tried in preference. One result was that before any clear verdict was officially established the aggressor was too far launched on his plan to be turned back by anything but force.

In the Manchurian and Ethiopian affairs, it was a question of preventing the forceful violation of the rights of peaceful states. The procedure was too hesitant, the power too unorganized. Something a great deal more clear-cut and vigorous would have been required to stop even flagrant illegality. These qualities will be still more necessary when it comes to inducing a strong state to forego the exercise of admitted legal rights. Yet that is inevitably involved in the revision of treaties and the correction of conditions which impose unreasonable hardships. Peaceful change will have to be possible even to the detriment of the powerful.

It will be the business of the regional associations to bring about such change as between their members, though they may in cases of special difficulty need the assistance of the universal organization, particularly if economic sanctions are employed. When, however, the adjustment becomes necessary between members of different regional associations, application will have to be made to the world organization. The suggestion was made in the last chapter that the first reference might be to the world court, for an authoritative statement of the existing law, and an indication of the derogation from that law needed to effect substantial settlement of the dispute where a mere equitable interpretation of existing rules would not be sufficient. This reference might take the form of a direct appeal by one of the parties, or, alternatively, a request to the court from the world organization for an advisory opinion. This opinion would go to the assembly of the world organization for adoption with or without modification, or for rejection, by majority vote. A simple majority should be adequate where the opinion is adopted without qualification, while a three-quarters or two-thirds majority might be required for amendment. Rejection of the court's proposals would be tantamount to a declaration in favor of applying existing law to the case. A derogation from the law differing from that recommended by the court, or voted by the assembly when none had been advised by the court, might properly be conditional on a larger majority, such as the three-fourths or two-thirds suggested above, by way of safeguard against ill-considered legislation.

If the community of states is to be equipped with agencies of economic and social control and development, as proposed in the chapter on Economic and Social Organization, changes in existing law and derogations from existing right will be implied in the creation of these agencies and will be carried out in detail in the course of their administration. Authority, for example, to order a lowering of tariffs, to annul import or export restrictions or exchange controls, or to impose a change in the conditions of labor, will mean a profound change in the international law which at present leaves to states unfettered liberty in these matters. Objection may be expected to placing such authority in the hands of technical bodies representing only a limited number of states. It will indeed be difficult enough to get consent to the exercise of powers like these by the general assembly or by such special conferences as, on the model of the International Labor Organization, may be given direction and supervision of the technical agencies. The alternative, however, would appear to be a passive acceptance of the prospect of repeated dislocations of international trade, with their attendant miseries, like those caused in the recent past by the use of unfettered national liberty. Only joint institutional control can save us from a position in which the general welfare is at the mercy of any economically powerful state. And experience has shown that joint control must not be subject to the rule of unanimity. If the supranational economic and social institutions are to operate in anything more than an advisory capacity, the greatest safeguard for national interest must be a right of appeal from administrative agencies to the policy-making bodies behind them, and a rule of qualified majority where the effect of proposed changes would bear hardly on one or more states.

Apart from the changes involved in the establishment and operation of institutions for the regulation of worldwide economic activity, and apart from equitable adjustments between particular states, there is great need for an agency entrusted with the careful but continuous definition and development of the general law binding upon nations. A large part of the time of foreign offices is taken up with attempts to redress wrongs suffered by their nationals in other countries. Yet this important and active branch of the law is a mass of uncertainties and contradictions. The same is true of the law regarding the jurisdiction of states over foreign ships in or near their ports and territorial waters, over foreigners for acts committed abroad, over claims against foreign states in their courts. Another subject crying out for rational legislation is the succession of states. When one state wholly or partially absorbs the territory of another, how far is it entitled to the rights, how far bound by the obligations of its predecessor? The catalogue could easily be enlarged; and while such uncertainties mar the general body of the law frequent disturbance can be expected in the community of states.

A suitable agency for this legislative work would be the Assembly of the universal association, which might well devote to it periodic special sessions. Patient preparatory work by committees of jurists would be necessary, and advisory opinions might be sought from the world court. The enactment of statutes on these matters, whether they be new law or merely declaratory, should not be made conditional on more than a three-fourths majority. It is understood, of course, that such enactments would be law without ratification by individual states.

How is our assembly to be constituted? In the early stages of this work, I was attracted by the idea of a body made up of representatives of the various regional associations. As a basis of discussion, I even specified the number of delegates that might come to the assembly from the association of European federations, from the inter-American association, from a league of Far Eastern countries, and from the Soviet Union. Much subsequent discussion and study have caused me to abandon this scheme. Its attraction lay most of all in its symmetry, but in this it exceeded the possibilities of the material. It assumed a cohesion within the regional associations which at least some of them will probably lack for a long time to come. It assumed also a clear-cut separation of the various associations; whereas they will inevitably overlap, with resulting duplication of representation in the world assembly. Finally, it gave no representation to nations not included in one or other of the regional associations.

For these reasons, it seems that the Assembly of the universal association will have to be formed, as the Assembly of the League of Nations has been, of delegations from the states. Any new federations will in this, as in most of their external relations, figure each as one state.

The first question to be decided here is whether representation shall be equal or graded according to the importance of the members. The champions of the equality of states will demand equal representation irrespective of population or economic resources. If they win their case, the new world association will be subject to the weakness in action which marked the League of Nations. Moreover, the high premium on statehood, which has impeded the advancement of human welfare in the past, will be continued. The will of the small nation, with a population of two millions, will count for as much as that of a national group numbering a hundred millions. The members providing the association with its main strength, and therefore its natural leaders, will either not be able to furnish leadership or will have to establish it by unrecognized means.

When the League of Nations was constituted, an attempt to avert these consequences was made by setting up an inner ring of members, the Council, where the great states would have a permanent majority. But the Assembly, in which all members were equally represented, was eventually able to secure for the small states a large majority even in the Council—a fact to which some commentators attribute the severance between the deliberations of the League and the power necessary to carry them into effect. The experience suggests either that the Council should be from the first and always composed exclusively of the Great Powers, or that there should be no such inner ring at all. If it consists only of the Great Powers, it is likely to absorb so much authority and to overshadow the Assembly to such an extent that for most substantial purposes the representation of the small states will become illusory. If, as before, its constitution provides for a minority of small countries, these seats may again become the object of a disruptive competition, and they may again be increased by successive amendments to a point where the original purpose of the Council is lost. If no Council is provided for—a proposal supported in this book—another way must be found to regularize that leadership which the great states will seek and which the association will need.

The problem abounds in difficulties, not the least of which is the psychological hostility to inequality. No alleged solution is free from objections. The suggestion is hazarded, however, that representation and voting power in some proportion to financial contribution would be worth trying. The financial contributions of the members should be determined from time to time by the assembly itself, using the economic ranking of the state as criterion. This was the procedure adopted after four years of experience in dividing the expenses of the League of Nations. In order to prevent an excessive preponderance of the richer countries, there should be a maximum voting power, say of three, and a minimum of one. This voting superiority would be made more acceptable to the weaker states if its exercise were limited to matters involving new expenditure and decisions of first rate importance to the Great Powers. The latter category would include measures affecting international trade, changes in the general law of nations, the creation of institutions exercising jurisdiction over states, and rules regarding the application of sanctions. Other items may have to be added to satisfy the members upon whose support the success of the association will principally depend. But if voluntary and serious co-operation is desired from the lesser countries, the shorter the list the better.

To replace the Council in the executive duties which it performed in the League of Nations, the Assembly would elect committees representing the nations and the functional organizations chiefly concerned in each major task. Thus, as in the International Labor Organization, associations of workers and employers might be called upon to send delegates to the bodies exercising economic and financial functions. Hitherto these bodies have, except for minor regulations, drawn up draft agreements which became binding only as they were ratified by the individual states. For the greater efficiency of the supranational community, the final competence to transform such drafts into laws binding upon all members should lie with the Assembly where, in matters of high importance, something more than a bare majority might be required to pass them.

What is here proposed amounts to the recognition and equipment of a World Commonwealth for the joint administration of interests which transcend national and regional boundaries. Over all its judicial, administrative and technical organs stands a unicameral Assembly which acts, within the limited range of business assigned to the Commonwealth in its constituent treaty, as a legislature. The essential differences between it and the Assembly of the League of Nations, which the new World Commonwealth will replace, are that its enactments will be binding upon the members without waiting for the slow and capricious process of ratification by each member acting independently, and that these enactments will be passed by simple or qualified majority.

CHAPTER XV

SUPRANATIONAL ADMINISTRATION

Unlike the resolutions on which the Pan American Union is based, the Covenant of the League of Nations contained no clause concerning the distribution of posts in the Secretariat among the states members. The two most active Great Powers in the foundation of the League were France and Great Britain, the official languages were French and English, the personnel was first assembled in London, and the permanent seat was at Geneva in the French-speaking part of Switzerland. All of these circumstances conspired to make the French and the English the two largest national and linguistic groups in the Secretariat—a fact which occasioned some resentment among the other members. From an early date the practice set in of diluting this original mass with the largest possible infusion of other nationalities. Posts at Geneva came in fact to be regarded as representation of the members in an international body, and there was a constant effort on the part of initially less favored states to win a representation in proportion to their political and economic importance and to their contribution to the work and finance of the League.

Behind this governmental rivalry for places, there was an indefeasible popular notion that members of the League Secretariat represented their states. The concept of an international civil service composed of persons working for the common interest of the entire League rather than for the advancement of any national cause in the League had very limited currency. Unfortunately the popular fallacy as to the function of the officials at Geneva was to some extent reflected and so perpetuated by their conduct in office. Frequently an official had been in one branch or another of government service for his state before coming to Geneva, and regarded himself and was regarded at home as temporarily seconded. This meant that he looked forward to continuing his career at home, possibly on a higher plane by reason of services rendered to his country at Geneva. National interest would inevitably tend to determine the direction of such a person's work, and this meant not only the subordination of the general purpose in his mind, but a lack of *esprit de corps* in the staff as a whole and a failure of that collective devotion to a common cause which should inspire any civil service. It was unhappily clear to anyone closely concerned in its activities that the Secretariat was in several important issues a house divided against itself. To understand this, it is only necessary to imagine what would happen if the civil service of a state were made up of delegates from the political constituencies.

In administration and in the conduct of research, as elsewhere, a permanent staff cannot avoid differences of opinion as to the course to be taken. These divergencies are the subject of discussion and the prevailing view determines practice. The differences here, however, are as to the comparative efficiency of various methods—a very different matter from division according to ideas, often instructed ideas, as to the bearing of one course or another on the claims of the states from which the officials come.

How is this tendency to carry forward national impulses and motives into international work to be overcome? Only by emphasizing in every possible way the fact that any international secretariat is the civil service of a community distinct from the individual communities which have associated in its formation. Carried to its logical conclusion this principle would mean that the personnel should be recruited without any regard to national distribution and with an eye solely to qualification for the work requiring to be done. Such an exclusive criterion would in itself involve some measure of distribution, for in some cases familiarity with terrain and language would be a qualification, while in other assignments a foreigner's impartiality might be a prime consideration.

Certainly it would not do to have a marked and permanent predominance of one or two nationalities in the Secretariat, for it would then be too much to ask of human nature not to suspect partiality, however denationalized in spirit the personnel might be. Yet it is doubtful whether more can safely be done, if the idea of representation of state interest is to be avoided, than to provide that in making appointments consideration should be given, other things being equal or nearly equal, to the expediency of a nationally heterogeneous Secretariat.

Certain specific aids to the international or supranational point of view on the part of officials can be added to this general directive. All positions should be for life, with retirement on pension fixed at a certain age. I can see no reason for the rotation of higher officials advocated by Mr. Buell and other writers. These are precisely the persons who will have most to do with shaping policy, and it is particularly in their case that the community motive must be insisted upon. The chance of developing the international mind in the central direction of regional or world organs of administration will be diminished if the highest officials know that their posts are only temporary and that they must look to their own countries for the continuance of their careers.

Part of the business of the assemblies, councils and committees to which international secretariats are responsible must be to examine charges of national partiality preferred against any higher official. They should be subject to dismissal on proof of such partiality, as on proof of any other form of inefficiency or corruption. Minor officers could be dealt with by the Secretary-General, perhaps assisted by a disciplinary council elected by the staff.

Where existing independent states are uniting to form federations, a federal citizenship will replace, or be added to, that of the individual states. Even where the original citizenship is retained by others, the civil servants of the new federations might well be required to give it up. There would be little difficulty in finding able men and women sufficiently devoted to the federal principle to make this sacrifice for the sake of permanent employment in the federal service.

The solution is less simple in the case of regional or world association not accompanied by the creation of a new citizenship. Is denationalization here compatible with finding the best persons for service in the regional or world secretariat? A special status might be established for the personnel, carrying with it an appropriate passport and all but civic rights in every associated country. Probably the sacrifice of nationality would even here produce no dearth of proper candidates for office. Indeed, this test of willingness to divest national allegiance, with its privileges, might operate as an excellent means of assuring the needed measure of internationalism in the permanent servants of the association of states. It would act as a deterrent chiefly in the case of nationals of the greater Powers, who would in any case tend to be overnumerous in the common secretariat.

Diplomatic privilege for the officials of international or supranational organizations is of doubtful utility. The case for maintaining in the modern world those immunities which in the past have been thought due to the mystical dignity of the sovereign state is itself not above controversy. International civil servants, like diplomatic agents, must be of a character that will require no exemption from the laws of any civilized country. If the law imposes a serious impediment upon the performance of an official's duty, that will normally be because he needs restraint and should not be occupying his post. The profession of diplomacy would probably render greater service to humanity if it were deflated by the removal of its medieval trappings, and only a clearly demonstrated necessity would justify adding to the ranks of those that wear them.

A World Commonwealth even in the first stage of development must have a considerable central secretariat coordinating the work of its various organs, keeping its records, assisting in the task of general supervision, and preparing agenda for meetings of a periodic Assembly. This staff must have a permanent seat for archives, library, and all the other equipment necessary for its extensive and varied functions. The suspicion and hostility aroused in some parts of the world by the League of 1919, and its final failure to keep the peace, have led a number of writers to advocate abandoning not only "League" as the name but Geneva as the seat of the proposed post-war association. But this concession to unfortunate associations surrounding the ill-fated peace establishment of Versailles means the sacrifice of a costly installation designed, after years of experience, for the precise purpose of serving as an international center: and situated in a country whose trilingual composition and long neutralization have made it the home of many international institutions. For more than a hundred years Switzerland has enjoyed sanctuary from the wars of Europe, and the failure of the League has not dissociated its name from the spirit of internationalism. The installation and the tradition should be maintained rather than abandoned in favor of a new setting.

If, however, an emotional opposition should develop at the next peace conference to the choice of Geneva, then the move should be in the direction of the United States. More than a little might be gained by establishing the administrative center of the new World Commonwealth in the territory of that Great Power which in the past has shown the strongest desire to avoid implication in and responsibility for the movement of world politics. Geographically, the United States is more central than Switzerland. And, if this move is contemplated, it would be well to place the headquarters of internationalism in that part of the United States which has been the source of most opposition to participation in a collective system. The presence of an international secretariat in Chicago might do much to alter that mentality which in 1920 repudiated Woodrow Wilson's League. The fortunes of the new institutions would not be prejudiced as the League was, by the Middle West's conviction of congenital European evil.

This change would have disadvantages. Unless Hitler succeeds in dominating Europe in a more or less permanent fashion, the United States will emerge from this war even more strongly entrenched than before in the position of greatest world Power economically and politically. Making it the center of the new association of nations would be likely to win some disfavor for this as an instrument of American hegemony. On any pretext the United States would be accused of taking advantage of the situation of the central offices to determine the policy of the association in its national interest. No such suspicion can be directed against a small state like Switzerland.

But whether Geneva or Chicago be chosen for headquarters, the Secretariat should not all be concentrated in one place. Institutions like the proposed World Bank and the World Trade Commission should be placed with their staff at an established center of commerce and finance, New York if Geneva is the general seat, London if Chicago replaces Geneva. The Commission on Migration and Settlement should be set up near one or other of the chief areas of possible settlement. In general the widest distribution consistent with efficient administration of the particular task of each organ and proper co-ordination with the other services should be the accepted policy. The more the different peoples see of the actual instrumentalities of internationalism, the more loyalty will these win. Geneva has much to recommend it as a general clearinghouse; but the concentration of League activities there meant not only a certain remoteness from the focus of many problems, but a widespread impression that the League was an exclusively European affair. A prudent measure of decentralization will cure these defects, especially if it be combined with the practice of sending officials frequently to see the territory and meet the human beings actually affected by their work. The academic seclusion which reduces all problems to paper formulas is at all costs to be avoided.

In addition to the measure of decentralization recommended above, and to frequent visits by officials to the people and areas affected by their work, much could be gained from placing permanent offices of the World Commonwealth in important regional centers. These would perform duties analogous to those now performed for states by their diplomatic or consular agencies in foreign countries. They would collect and disseminate information of a political, economic and social character and, in general, maintain a useful liaison between the universal and the regional associations.

As a means of providing qualified candidates for the civil service of this Commonwealth, an International Staff College should be set up at the general headquarters. Competitive examinations should be held at intervals throughout the world for the selection of students. A scheme of fellowships, financed not by the individual states but by the World Commonwealth, would provide assistance for successful aspirants unable to pay their own way. The College would perform a useful function, not only in providing expert training but in inducing the spirit of impartial world citizenship. Once under way, this system should be made the normal process of recruitment, state governments being relieved of any part in appointments.

CHAPTER XVI

COLONIES AND MANDATES

Any design for the prevention of war, whether it takes the form of league or federation, must eventually deal with the colonial possessions of the states to be associated. Rightly or wrongly, the fact that some states have many of these while others have few or none is a source of constant discontent and complaint. Some colonies are important producers of food and raw materials and possession of them may therefore promise a supply not to be cut off by the arbitrary decision of some foreign authority. Nations which regard intermittent war as the normal condition of humanity are therefore particularly likely to covet such dependencies. So long, indeed, as the world is subject to violent disturbance by aggressors, even the most peaceful-minded people is apt to regard colonies as an important element of economic or strategic defense and to turn a deaf ear to proposals for sharing them.

Colonies also offer prospects of careers for the energetic youth of the metropolis. The call to acquire them thus makes a ready and stirring appeal to the best military material in the nation.

Finally, as bases for land, naval or air forces, colonies may serve to protect lines of commerce and to extend the power and influence of the mother-country far beyond its natural boundaries.

These reasons are enough to explain why the acquisition of colonies has become an object in itself, quite apart from their material value. Their possession has come to be associated with power and prestige, and nations are willing to commit violent and bloody aggression for areas of desert. Nations growing to greatness feel that they have an inherent right to a share in these *indicia* of might.

Any substantial justification for claims to colonies would

be automatically removed by the establishment of such agencies of world government as would secure equitable distribution of primary commodities and prevent war. Under such conditions the size and power of nations would have even less bearing on the welfare of their inhabitants than they have now, and the artificial prestige associated with dependencies would in time disappear. But the existing inequality of states in this respect is one of the obstacles to the establishment of agencies of world government which, failing a preliminary equalization, are apt to be looked upon as devices for the preservation of an inequitable *status quo*. The possessors are also likely to be regarded with jealousy because they will be thought to have better safeguards for continued security and welfare in the event of the supranational organization breaking down.

To share out the colonies as a step preliminary to federation or reconstituted and reformed league would involve dislocations as disastrous as they would be absurd. The alternative appears to be their assignment to the federation or league for administration.

The advocates of federation are agreed that colonies must henceforth be considered a trust, with the inhabitants as primary beneficiaries, and brought under the general principles of the mandate system, reinforced by the addition of direct powers of investigation and sanctions for breach of trust. Most of them shrink, however, from an outright transfer to the federation. With some this is due to a political calculation; they do not wish to frighten off the possessors from joining their association by the appearance of too much sacrifice. It may be questioned whether these planners make sufficient concession to the "have-nots" invited to membership, who may well be dissatisfied with anything less than a surrender of colonial sovereignty by the present holders. And if a really effective control is vested in the central authority, the residue of insubstantial sovereignty will be small solace to the titularies.

A more significant reason advanced by other writers who oppose transfer is the risk involved in shifting the actual administration on the spot from the experienced hands of the present colonial services. But such a consequence need not follow a surrender of sovereignty to a supranational authority. Even those who advocate leaving the colonies with their present owners, subject to supervision in the general interest, recommend that the national colonial service be thrown open to foreigners. This is all that need be done in any case. After transfer of the legal sovereignty to the new collectivity, the personnel and organization now functioning should be gradually internationalized. To uproot and replace them at once would be folly under any system.

The best solution of the colonial problem is, then, the surrender of what is known as sovereignty to the new collective organization, coupled with administration through the existing services. These services would at once become responsible to the supranational authority and vacancies would be filled by examination open to all nationals of the associated states. All who deal with this subject agree that the colonies are to cease serving the particular interest of any state and are to be administered henceforth in the general interest. Admittedly also the employment which they offer to any non-native personnel should be open to all citizens of the contemplated association of states. Collective funds are to be expended in colonial public works, in the further development of industry, and in the improvement of social and sanitary conditions. To leave the so-called sovereignty where it now resides would be to recognize a surviving special interest in particular states. This would be incompatible with the essential purposes of the new regime, and it would lead to disputes about residuary powers and rights which, in addition to impeding progressive administration of backward areas, would weaken the superstate association as a whole.

Those who would preserve individual state titles to colonies are confronted with a difficult problem in Germany's claim to restoration of at least some of the dependencies which belonged to her before 1914. In his very thoughtful book *The United States of Europe,* Alfred Bingham holds that the administration of her former colonies should be at least nominally returned to Germany. In *A Federation for Western Europe,* Ivor Jennings suggests the return of the mandated territories to the Reich "as a possibility, though a very remote possibility." These authors, like many others, not only recognize the psychological importance of the claim but admit its inherent equity in a world which permits individual states to have colonies. But the suggested restoration would arouse fears and antipathies not only in Africa, but in the Pacific as well. It would mean dislocation and confusion for the sake of what would be a retrograde step in the relations between "civilized" states and native populations. If there is to be a change, with its accompanying risks, let it be in a forward direction. Immediate internationalization in form and principle, and gradual internationalization in personnel, remove the grounds for the German claim, give the most concrete and dependable expression to the doctrine of trusteeship, and secure, with the least disturbance of established usage, the most direct guaranty of that general interest which is now the declared purpose of colonial administration.

Plans of European federation provide for a federal commission to supervise administration and to accelerate development in colonial areas. The building of roads and other public works, the establishment or expansion of industry, the scientific improvement of agriculture, the creation and extension of public health services—all such measures are regarded as being equally in the interest of Europe and of the native populations. With these activities in progress, an outlet will be provided for European industries faced with the necessity of contracting from a war to a peace economy. Pushed up to a scale commensurate with the need and the opportunity, they would also provide an outlet for the glut of manpower which will follow on demobilization and the shrinking of production for national war use.

Such functions could not be performed without a very considerable secretarial and technical staff and close collaboration between the national colonial offices. They would also involve the intimate co-operation of the general economic and financial services of the federation. They point almost inevitably to the gradual fusion of colonial offices in one large department of the supranational government. A mere commission, whether of experts or political personages, reporting to that government, is not enough. Colonial administration will be a task of the first magnitude, and those charged with it must form an integral part of the supranational authority. The proposal to make over all dependencies not ready for immediate self-government, which has been adopted here, means that the fusion would take place at an earlier stage. It follows closely on the shifting of responsibility in the colonial services away from national governments to the supranational association. It of course involves problems of personnel and organization that can hardly be solved without opposition and friction. They will be child's play, however, compared with the problems of organization for war; and since they are part of the alternative to war this is the comparison which should be kept in mind.

The disadvantage of shifting the loyalty of colonial populations from their present regimes to a new authority has been exaggerated by writers who are themselves nationals of colonial powers. There would be no sudden change in the visible agents of authority or in their practice; and it has yet to be proved that a change in the relatively remote and abstract incidence of sovereignty would, in the native mind, constitute a major calamity. It would clearly mean more to the European settlers, who are of course an important and vocal part of the populations concerned. They would lose the privileged position which they now occupy as citizens of the governing state. But such privilege is clearly incompatible with the now recognized principle of trusteeship exercised for the benefit of the inhabitants, offering equal opportunity to all residents. Changes such as these will in some cases involve unwilling emotional adjustments; but they are not likely to bulk large among the problems of post-war reconstruction.

Some of the studies which deal with the colonial problem treat it as an important aspect of the federalization of Europe, and it is to the joint European authority that they assign general supervision over the dependencies of all the participating states. They thus make a separation between colonies and mandates, though they would apply the same principles, for the existing mandates are left to a re-established world league. This treatment is hardly adapted to the recognition of universal interest in the commerce and in the progress of the colonial territories. Nor does it take into account the important fact that many of the European dependencies lie within the regional boundaries of the Pan American or the Far Eastern group, and that these groups accordingly have an undeniable claim to a share in the supervision of their development. Considerations such as these point to what we have called the World Commonwealth as the final authority for the administration of the colonies as well as of the mandates. Not merely the principles but the system of administration should be unified, the word "colony" should disappear, and all of these trust territories be known as mandates.

What is proposed here, then, is that the colonial commission which so many of the federationists attach to their federal government of Europe should find its place under another name among the institutions of the World Commonwealth. The Mandates Commission, as an agency of the Commonwealth and reporting to its Assembly, would employ all necessary inspectors in the territories and would communicate advice and criticism directly to the state governments provisionally carrying on the government there. The expression "provisionally carrying on" is used intentionally. It would be unwise to terminate immediately the control and responsibility of the present colonial or mandate Powers; but the process of internationalization of personnel and authority should begin at once, and its logical conclusion is the gradual displacement of those Powers and the assumption of direct and complete responsibility by the World Commonwealth. As rapidly as prudence will permit foreign personnel will be replaced by officers drawn from the territorial populations themselves.

The completion of this process will of course render the term "mandate" even more technically inaccurate than it has been in the League system. The World Commonwealth will at that point not be using mandatory states for the fulfillment of its mission in the politically undeveloped territories, and the Mandates Commission should logically become a Commission for Territorial Administration. In this connection, however, the precise shading of terminology is of little importance.

What may be of importance is the final disposal of the hitherto vexed question of sovereignty. Under the League of Nations, the controversy never ceased raging as to whether sovereignty in the mandates belonged to the League, the mandated community, or the mandatory state. Enough could be said in favor of the sovereignty of the mandatory state to provide formal justification for legislative or administrative measures that suggested monopoly rather than mandate or trust. In earlier paragraphs of this chapter emphasis is laid on the surrender of so-called sovereignty to the World Commonwealth, but the historical associations of the word, and above all the legal absolutism connected with it, make it an unsuitable description of the authority to be exercised by the World Commonwealth. It would be better to recognize that we have here a new institution to which the traditional terminology of constitutional and international law is not applicable. If an analogy must be found, guardianship would be more suitable. The essential thing is to emphasize that the function of the World Commonwealth in relation to these communities is to encourage and safeguard their advancement toward political maturity, as a guardian fosters the development of his ward, and in the meantime to secure for them the fullest possible participation in the commercial and social community of nations.

Not all of the existing colonies should come under the administration of the World Commonwealth. Many of them are in a sufficiently advanced stage of development to become at once members of a regional association or the World Commonwealth, or of both. Only those communities which are clearly incapable of participation in these groups on a footing at least approximating equality should be kept in a position of tutelage. The same principle would apply to the present mandates.

CHAPTER XVII

WORLD ORDER

In the "Atlantic Charter" of August 14, 1941, the President of the United States and the Prime Minister of Great Britain "jointly pledged their countries to the final destruction of the Nazi tyranny." Those are the words of Mr. Churchill when, ten days later, he broadcast his account of the meeting. They also undertook to follow, after that victory, an eight-point program of political and economic collaboration for the peace and prosperity of all peoples.

The "Atlantic Charter" is of course ridiculed for its vagueness by the agencies of Axis propaganda. Some of our own people, having no faith in internationalism, point with skepticism to its silence on the methods by which the high aims so dramatically announced are to be attained.

Yet, with all its lack of definition, the joint declaration brings new and needed strength to those who in the midst of war are striving to keep alive the idea of supranational organization as the path of peace and civilized progress. It came at an opportune moment, when the enthusiasm for new leagues and federations which marked the early days of the war was giving way to a wave of pessimism. The too rosy visions of a new world were being driven into the background by disastrous events, and a reaction calling itself by the flattering name of "realism" had set in against all planning. The growing contempt for evangelical "blueprints" threatened to stifle all thought of rehabilitating and improving the peace machinery of the 'twenties.

The President and the Prime Minister have set a task for those who practice or teach, with patience and sobriety, the arts or sciences of politics and economics. What are the practical implications of the aims which they have proclaimed on behalf of the American and British peoples? What means, what institutions, are best calculated to transform their common vision into a reality?

Those who set about answering these questions will find that the League of Nations was not a wasted effort. Looking back upon its operation, they may well be impressed by how much it did and how near it came to doing infinitely more. They will find in its experience not only hope but instruction for the future.

It may be conceded with little argument that, given good will and courage on the part of its principal members, the League was well enough designed to produce many of the results expected of it. A common diagnosis of its failure is that this was due to the combined stupidity and selfishness of the Great Powers, rather than any defect of machinery. It is a truism that, with intelligence and devotion, great ends may be achieved with the weakest organization. But this admission does not carry us very far. The difference between good and bad machinery is that the former eliminates many strains and is strong enough to withstand those that cannot be eliminated. It can tide over temporary failures of good will and operate against manifestations of bad will. Judged by this standard the League machinery was weak.

The weaknesses of the League which figure most prominently in the many studies that have been devoted to its work are four in number:

1) That it had no means at its direct disposal for the enforcement of decisions;

2) That it had no compulsory jurisdiction in the settlement of disputes;

3) That it had no adequate provision for peaceful change;

4) That it had no adequate machinery of economic cooperation.

This finding argues the necessity of reducing the sovereignty of individual states in the economic as in the political sphere. It has pointed many men engaged in practical affairs, as well as many theorists, to something in the nature of federal organization with a common police, a supreme court, a legislative and governing body, and common economic agencies for advice and control. Federalism became a word to conjure with; and the reasons are not far to seek. It is a familiar fact that by federal union highly individualized groups have achieved united strength, security against external aggression, and peaceful and prosperous mutual relations, while retaining a satisfactory measure of local autonomy.

It is, however, an important truth that, as Georges Scelle points out,[1] successful federation presupposes a preliminary sense of community among the units to be federated and a voluntary disposition toward at least limited union. Federal union cannot, in other words, be imposed simply because it is rationally indicated. The criticism advanced against such plans as that of Clarence Streit—that they seek to bring about at once and over centuries of separatism a revolutionary abdication of national prerogatives—is a valid one.

That is not to say that we cannot borrow some of the features of federalism for wider international use. But we may have to resign ourselves to leaving to the nations concerned some of the inconvenient liberties maintained by members of that looser type of association technically known as confederation. In Europe, where there is the greatest need of closer association, and where the possibility has been most discussed, there will in the most favorable circumstances be obstacles of psychology as well as of vested interest to any type of union, and it seems elementary wisdom to begin with workable and acceptable approximations rather than institutions satisfying the classical definitions. We may agree that the goal is federation, but we may have to be satisfied at first with quasi-federal machinery.

We shall also have to content ourselves with something far short of universal federation. Distance has been reduced in terms of days and hours by modern invention, but the psychological gaps between nations have not been closed. There have been tentative approaches toward federation in limited areas, as in Scandinavia, the Baltic States, and in

[1] "Le Problème du Fédéralisme," *Politique Etrangère*, April 1940. See Chapter IV above for summary.

the Balkans; and it will be well to take full advantage of these tendencies when the opportunity comes. But even where there is a fundamental identity of political theory, ingrained habits of independence and convictions of self-sufficiency will continue in some cases to withstand the biddings of expediency.

The proposal of a single federal union for Europe, launched by Coudenhove-Kalergi and taken up by Briand, has not stood very well the subsequent examination in which practical politicians have joined with the theorists. The tendency now is to plan for parallel federations each composed of states already linked closely by geography, economics, and habits of living. A number of contemporary studies use some of the elements of the balance-of-power system—a fact which discredits them with some readers. Distaste for anything savoring of a method which has so signally failed in late years to keep the peace of Europe is another manifestation of the passion for clear-cut types of political association in a context which calls for the combination of workable features of different types. A balance of federations, if left to itself, would be as unstable as the balance of states has proved to be. Within a co-ordinating organization, on the other hand, such a balance may be, not the lesser of evils, but a positive aid to success. That is how it is employed, for example in the studies by Scelle and by Buell, where the union of smaller states about Germany is advocated as a means of meeting any renewed ambition in that country to dominate the reorganized Europe.

From the gropings of statesmen and political scientists toward a workable scheme of world organization there emerges a trend in the direction of a combination of special groups, held together by geographical or other bonds, with a general association for purposes of an essentially universal character. The special groups need not have, and are almost certain not to have, the same internal mechanism of joint government or co-operation. We must contemplate a world order embracing associations of states varying all the way from close-knit federal unions in some parts of

Europe to the something less than confederation of Pan America. Some members of these associations will be participants also in groups like the British Commonwealth, which defy geographical classification. The linking together of such unlikes into a workable unity is going to require creative imagination disciplined but not fettered by past experience. This is the great task for the contemporary science and practice of politics. There is no good reason to suppose that it exceeds the powers of man. Julian Huxley says in an article already referred to, "War is a phenomenon on a par with duelling and religious persecution. These have dropped out of civilized societies without any alteration in the genetic basis of human nature; and the same can be accomplished for war."[2] The elimination of war and the establishment of a firm world order are one and the same thing.

The type of world organization to which our argument runs is, then, neither universal federation nor yet simply league. It combines the beginnings of a World Commonwealth with other, limited, groupings of states around regional or other special interests. The World Commonwealth admits all political communities which its Assembly deems fit for membership. Its functions are less numerous than were those of the League of Nations; but within their scope it is given more authority to decide and to act. Many of the problems with which the League attempted unsuccessfully to deal will be the business of the more limited groups. This, it is submitted, is the arrangement best adapted to the infinite variety and the ethnical and geographical distribution of the problems to be met. It combines the centralization of general direction with decentralization of detailed control—a principle proved in democratic national government.

Two well defined regional groups already exist. They are the inter-American system and the Union of Soviet Socialist Republics. Organization for Europe, apart from that now being imposed (it is to be hoped only temporarily)

[2] "Science, War and Reconstruction," *Science*, New York, February 16, 1940.

by Nazi Germany, is still in the planning stage, and must await the outcome of the present war. There is moreover, as anyone who has read the preceding chapters will be abundantly aware, a great diversity in the plans. A single federation of that continent is, however, a remote prospect. There seems to be some possibility of a number of federal or quasi-federal unions, and it may be that a looser organization, which Sir Walter Layton drafts as a Confederation of Europe,[3] can be formed to make a working community of the whole. A Far Eastern association, sketched in an earlier chapter as an Eastern League, has yet to be called into existence.

These four groups, two already constituted and two potential only, are the necessary minimum of regional organization. Many nations lie outside their scope. They do not touch the Near East, where Turkey, Persia, Egypt and other states must participate in any durable world order. Australia, South Africa and New Zealand fall outside their boundaries. There are rough edges everywhere.

As for the Near East, there has been talk of a Mohammedan League stretching from the European frontiers of Turkey over North Africa and down to parts of India. South Africa, Australia and New Zealand will probably cling to their membership in the British Commonwealth. In any case, all of these countries will be eligible for participation in the World Commonwealth, which for some nations may have to fill the place of regional association.

Since the World Commonwealth envisaged here has no collective armed force at its immediate disposal, the objection may be raised that the whole plan makes no adequate provision for the danger of war between regions, that it indeed divides the world into bigger and stronger embattled groups. Some justice may be admitted in the criticism without abandoning the view that the plan is the best that can be hoped for in the near future. In partial rebuttal, however, it may be pointed out that much of the risk will be averted by the regional organization itself. The great strug-

[3] *Peace Aims,* a *News-Chronicle* pamphlet, London, 1940.

gles which have rocked the world in the last half-century had their origin in conflicts within the areas marked out. Regional machinery for peaceful settlement could have prevented them from spreading. Finally, the chances of conflict between these areas will be reduced by the removal of causes of friction through the intelligent operation of the universal legislative, judicial, economic and social agencies maintained by the World Commonwealth.

Most of these agencies have been described in earlier chapters. The description is summarized in what follows, and some other institutions are added which may be carried on, with little if any alteration, from the beginning made under the League of Nations:

1) An Assembly composed of delegates from each member of the Commonwealth. The original members of the Commonwealth would be all states accepting an invitation to be issued by the general peace conference held after a suitable interval following the cessation of hostilities in the present war. Thereafter new members would be admitted by two-thirds vote of the Assembly. This is the body which, acting by majority, draws up the statutes governing the administration of interregional interests, appoints the personnel of the various organs of the World Commonwealth, establishes its budget and supervises its expenditure, determines general policy and reviews its execution, and enacts necessary reforms in the law of nations.

2) A World Court, with compulsory jurisdiction in interregional disputes, and acting as the preliminary forum in claims for changes in the law of nations.

3) An Economic and Financial Organization, embracing Trade, Development, and Migration Commissions, and a Central Bank. The function of these institutions, assisted by the research staff of the general secretariat, would be to regulate the production and distribution of raw materials and food, control the flow of interregional investment and migration, assist in the development of backward areas, maintain so far as possible a stable ratio between the world's

currencies and secure the gradual reduction of barriers to world trade.

4) A Social Organization embracing the International Labor Organization with its function of improving all working conditions, together with Health and Social Services to carry on the work of the League of Nations in checking epidemics and combating drug and white-slave traffics and to co-operate in the development work of the Economic and Financial Organization.

5) A Territorial Administration Commission to continue, with new powers of direct investigation on the spot, the supervision of conditions in the territories still under the mandates of 1919, together with the colonies to be surrendered to the World Commonwealth, and to ensure the development of all these communities toward autonomy.

6) A Commission on Transit and Communications to carry on the much needed co-ordination in this field inaugurated by the similar organization under the League of Nations. The various conventions governing the maintenance and use of international waterways will have to be revised and reinstated with the appropriate agencies of control and regulation. The same is true of rail and air traffic between states. All of this essentially joint legislation and administration, including the work of the International Commission for Air Navigation established by the Paris Convention of 1919, has broad interregional aspects which should be brought together under the jurisdiction of the World Commonwealth.

7) A Commission on Intellectual Co-operation to continue the work of the League in the exchange of scientific knowledge and personnel, and the protection of the rights of intellectual workers in the product of their labors. This body should also take charge of the very necessary popular education in internationalism. An important part of this task would be the depiction by film, radio and pamphlet, of the far-reaching activities of the World Commonwealth.

Some advocates of supranational organization in these days would make it the first business of a constituent congress to draw up a new bill of human rights and provide for its enforcement by the collective authority. The rights usually enumerated are freedom of religion, speech, movement and association; security from secret legal process; education, employment, food, clothing and shelter. Their realization would be equivalent to pretty complete socialization everywhere. In his *World Order,* H. G. Wells insists that "we have to collectivize the world as one system with practically everyone playing a reasonably satisfying part in it," and again, "What is needed, as the alternative to a long dark age, is a revolution to outright world-socialism, with a sustained insistence on law based on a fuller restatement of the personal rights of man, plus freedom of speech, criticism and publication and a sedulous expansion of the educational organization."

Those who hold this doctrine tell us that until these things are accomplished it will be useless to devise or attempt to establish any supranational system of peace and co-operation. They appear also to believe that once the individual is assured of his fundamental right to freedom, sustenance, and development, world order will be *ipso facto* established. For the most part, therefore, they refrain from drafting any constitutional framework for that order.

All of us who adhere to democracy may agree that the specified liberties and rights are highly desirable. But how are they to be attained? By action within the separate states? That cannot proceed at an equal pace, nor can it procure the benefits expected without international exchange and collaboration. Probably no country can achieve complete autarchy, and most countries cannot even approach it. A spontaneous world revolution aiming not only at the abolition of privilege, class, monopoly, but at the suppression of political boundaries and the fusion of all peoples into one society is as inconceivable as the immediate perfection of civilization in every corner of the globe. Socialization in state compartments will not necessarily bring with it the cessation of interstate rivalry. The socialist nation, while suppressing the profit motive among its citizens, may continue to be aggressively acquisitive as a people. Even if it be admitted for the sake of argument that socialism is a condition of peace, it does not follow that it is the sole condition.

If it cannot be assumed that the present war will destroy all the things that have kept men apart and blend them into one perfect community, we must face the prospect of a world still divided into groups—however different in size and composition from those now existing—clinging to a large measure of autonomy, and differing greatly in resources, industrial and social development, and political organization. Unless we are content to contemplate anarchy in their relations, anarchy which will impede their progress and impair the welfare of the individual citizen, we must devise new means of reconciling their conflicts and securing their active co-operation. The improvement of the lot of the individual within his group and the improvement of relations between the groups are interdependent and must proceed *pari passu*.

This book is dedicated to the thesis that peace is not incompatible with the existence of separate political communities. The development of the nation-state did not await the dissolution of clans or feudal units; it was superimposed, and only gradually did it complete their subordination to itself. The state machinery for the administration of common interests and enforcement of the common law did not await a unanimous will to peace within the state. If it had, it would still be waiting. Its creation required the support of the strongest individual or group, but once established its operation extended the sense of community and the will to peace among the citizenry.

Similarly, the establishment of supranational institutions is conditional on the agreement of a dominant group of states. The operation of such institutions, once they have been created, will extend the will to world peace and the sense of world community. It is to this method, which is essentially gradual, that we must look for the reduction of the state to its proper place in human affairs, rather than to a spontaneous world revolution sweeping away in a tidal wave of brotherhood the separatism of centuries. No political miracle of that magnitude waits round the corner.

BIBLIOGRAPHY

(1) BOOKS

Sir Norman Angell, *For What Do We Fight?*, New York, Harper, 1940.

Alfred M. Bingham, *The United States of Europe*, New York, Duell, Sloan and Pearce, 1940.

Raymond Leslie Buell, *Isolated America*, New York, Knopf, 1940.

George Catlin, *Anglo-Saxony*, New York, Macmillan, 1939.

J. B. Condliffe, *The Reconstruction of World Trade*, Norton, New York, 1940.

Count Coudenhove-Kalergi, *Pan-Europa*, New York, 1926.

W. B. Curry, *The Case for Federal Union*, London, Penguin, 1939.

Lionel Curtis, *Civitas Dei*, London, Oxford University Press, 1938.

J. F. Dulles, *War, Peace and Change*, New York, Harper, 1939.

F. S. Dunn, *Peaceful Change*, New York, Council on Foreign Relations, 1937.

Graeme K. Howard, *America and a New World Order*, New York, 1940.

International Institute of Intellectual Co-operation, *Peaceful Change*, Paris, 1938.

W. Ivor Jennings, *A Federation for Western Europe*, New York, Macmillan, 1940.

Harold Laski, *Where Do We Go from Here?*, New York, Viking Press, 1940.

R. W. Mackay, *Peace Aims and the New Order*, London, Michael Joseph, 1941.

J. E. Mcade, *Economic Bases of a Durable Peace*, London, Oxford University Press, 1940.

Kate Mitchell and W. L. Holland, *Problems of the Pacific, 1939*, New York, Institute of Pacific Relations, 1940.

Oscar Newfang, *World Federation*, New York, Barnes and Noble, 1939.

Harold Nicolson, *Why Britain Is at War*, London, Penguin, 1939.

Nathaniel Peffer, *Prerequisites to Peace in the Far East*, New York, Institute of Pacific Relations, 1940.

William Rappard, *The Quest for Peace Since the World War*, Cambridge, Mass., Harvard University Press, 1940.

J. F. Rippy, *Latin America in World Politics*, 3rd ed., New York, Knopf, 1940.

Eugene Staley, *World Economy in Transition*, New York, Council on Foreign Relations, 1939.

Clarence Streit, *Union Now*, 1939; and *Union Now with Britain*, 1941, New York, Harper.
James P. Warburg, *Peace in Our Time*, New York, Harper, 1940.
H. G. Wells, *New World Order*, New York, Knopf, 1940.
H. M. Wriston, *Prepare for Peace*, New York, Harper, 1941.

(2) ARTICLES AND PAMPHLETS

Annals of the American Academy of Political and Social Science, *When War Ends*, July 1940, and *The New World Order*, July 1941, Philadelphia.
Sir William Beveridge, *Peace by Federation*, Federal Union, London, 1940.
H. Brailsford, *Can Europe Federate?*, The New Republic, March 18, 1940.
A. J. B., *The German "New Order" in Europe*, The Bulletin of International News, London, January 25, 1941.
Viscount Cecil, *A Real Peace*, London, Hamish Hamilton, 1941.
Grenville Clark, *A Memorandum . . . Containing a Proposal for a Federation of Free Peoples*, New York, January 1940.
Commission to Study the Organization of Peace, *Preliminary Report and Monographs*, International Conciliation, No. 369, April 1941.
Count Coudenhove-Kalergi, *Can Europe Unite?*, Christian Science Monitor Magazine, December 2, 1939.
P. F. Drucker, *Germany's Plans for Europe*, Harper's Magazine, November, 1940.
F. W. Eggleston, *Long-Term Aims of the War*, Austral-Asiatic Bulletin, December-January 1939-1940.
Federal Council of the Churches of Christ in America, *A Just and Durable Peace*, 297 Fourth Ave., New York, April 1941.
Fortune Round Table, No. 8, February 1941, *Peace Aims*.
Geneva Research Center, *Official Statements of War and Peace Aims*, December 1940.
G. W. Guillebaud, *Hitler's New Economic Order for Europe*, The Economic Journal, December 1940.
Alvin Hansen, *Hemisphere Solidarity*, Foreign Affairs, October 1940.
Julian Huxley, *Science, War and Reconstruction*, Science, New York, February 16, 1940.
P. F. Irvine, *The Implications of Australian War Aims*, The Australian Quarterly, December 1939.
Sir Walter Layton, *Peace Aims*, News-Chronicle pamphlet, London, 1940.
William P. Maddox, *European Plans for World Order*, American Academy of Political and Social Science, Philadelphia, 1940.

Jacques Maritain, *Europe and the Federal Idea,* The Commonweal, April 19 and 26, 1940.
Felix Morley, *The Formula of Federation,* Asia, June 1940.
Harold Nicolson, *Allied War Aims,* The New Republic, February 20, 1940.
William Rappard, *Fédéralisme International,* L'Esprit International, Paris, January 1940.
Denis Saurat, *French Aims,* The Fortnightly, London, April 1940.
Georges Scelle, *Le Problème du Fédéralisme,* Politique Etrangère, Paris, April 1940.
Hans Schmidt, *Germany—The Voice from Within,* Harper's Magazine, June 1940.
General Smuts, *Prospects of War and Peace,* British Library of Information, New York, 1940.
Clarence Streit, *For Mutual Advantage,* Atlantic Monthly, November 1940.
Quincy Wright, *International Law and the World Order,* Harris Foundation, 1940, University of Chicago Press.

INDEX

Aaland Islands, dispute over, 15
Agricultural commodities, 121
Air forces, 38
Air Navigation Convention of Paris, 160
Albania, 17
American Institute of International Law, 65
Anglo-American collaboration
  Atlantic Charter, 10, 11, 97, 185
  defense, 91
  world organization, 92, 93, 95, 143, 144
Anglo-French union, 35-41, 48
Anglo-Japanese Alliance, 25
Annals of the American Academy of Political and Social Science, 124 *footnote*, 129
Anschluss, 20
Anti-Axis nations
  purpose common to, 5
  war aims, 10
Arbitration
  and conciliation, 63, 68, 152
  compulsory, 13
  Permanent Court of, 98
  submission to, 100
Argentine Anti-War Pact, 65
Atlantic Charter, 10, 11, 97, 185
Austral-Asiatic Bulletin, 52
Australia
  Board Report, 131
  defense of Southern Asia, 74
  on sanctions, 21
  regional grouping, 80
Austria
  economic dislocation of, 16, 122
  invasion of, 23
Axis Powers,
  in Latin America, 62
  world domination of, 23, 89

Bank of International Settlements, 35, 128

Behring Sea Fur Seals Case, 148
Beveridge, Sir William, *Peace by Federation*, 49
Bicameral system, 155
Bingham, Alfred M., *The United States of Europe*, 52, 179
Blaine, James, Conference of American Republics, 58
Bogota Conference of 1943, 69
Bolivar, Simon, 58
Bonn, Dr. Moritz, "The New World Order," 124 *footnote*, 129, 130
Briand, Aristide
  European federal union plan, 20, 29, 42, 188
  Locarno Agreements, 19
Briand-Kellogg Pact, 27, 100
British
  Commonwealth, 8, 189, 190
  Malaya, 74
  nations, 4, 8, 18
  navy, 118
Bruce, Stanley, League report, 131, 132
Bryan Treaties, 153
Buell, Raymond Leslie, *Isolated America*, 33, 34, 52, 53, 77, 78, 139, 172, 188
Buenos Aires Convention of 1936, 59, 67
Bulgaria, 15
Burma, 74
Bustamante Code of Private International Law, 66

Canada sanctions, 21, 22
Carnegie
  Andrew, 57
  Endowment for International Peace, 127 *footnote*
Cartels, 39
Central American Court of Justice, 65

201

Chamberlain, Sir Austen, 19
China
   appeal to League, 20
   Far Eastern settlement, 73, 74
Churchill, Winston, 8, 10, 185
Civitas Dei, 31, 42, 44
Clark, Grenville, *Memorandum on a Federation of Free Peoples*, 53
Colijn, Hendrik, 132
Collective security, 4, 21, 71
Colonial
   administration, 39, 178, 179, 181, 182
   claims, 177, 179
   Commission, 39
   doctrine of trusteeship, 39, 78, 180, 181
   possessions, 71
Commercial Bureau of the American Republics, 58
Commission of American Jurists, 65
Commission of Inquiry for European Union, 30
Commission on Migration and Settlement, 35, 175
Communism, 21
Conciliation
   and arbitration, 152, 153
   Argentine Anti-War Pact, 65
   commissions, 64
   Convention, 64
Condliffe, J. B., 116, 120, 123, 125
   footnotes, 126, 130
Confederation of Europe, 190
Conference of Ambassadors, 17
Congress of Panama, 141
Constitution of United States, 156
Continental Army, 142
Corfu, 17
Coudenhove-Kalergi, Count, 29, 188
Council of League, 14, 17, 154, 167, 168
Covenant of League, 12, 14, 15, 18, 26, 102, 160, 161, 162, 168, 170
Credit expansion, 121
Curtis, Lionel
   Civitas Dei, 31, 42, 43
Customs union, 20, 31, 83

Daladier, Premier, 50
Danzig, 15, 23
Davies, Lord, *The Problem of the Twentieth Century*, 137
Dawes Plan, 19, 120
Declaration of Lima, 59
Depression, 26
Disarmament
   Conference, 21
   problem of, 10, 38, 71, 97
   Washington Conference, 25
Draft Treaty of 1923, 18

Eastern League, 79, 80, 82
Economic
   agency for reconstruction, 38
   authority, 165
   breakdown, 124
   Conference, Geneva, 1927, 20
   council, Staley suggestion for, 132
   needs and forces, 34
   organization, 35
   problem
      national and international, 126
      subordination to political, 30
   relations, 117
   sanctions, 102
Economic Analysis and Policy, 125, 128
Economic Bases of a Durable Peace, 125, 128
Economic Organization of Peace, The, 127
Eden, Anthony, 9, 124
Eggleston, F. W., "Long-Term Aims of the War," 52
Encirclement, 18
Equality, principle of, 95
Ethiopia, 21, 164
Eugenics and Homoculture, 63
Europe
   Briand's policy, 20
   federalization of, 37
   German plans for, 83, 86
   multi-federal plans, 33
   superstate organization, 143
   weakness of League, 36
Europe and the Federal Idea, 50

INDEX

European
  Assembly, 37
  Commission of the Danube, 160
  Conference, 29
  Council, 37
  federation, 37, 180
  police agency, 38
  union, 30, 49, 87
Extraterritoriality, 73

Far East in a New World Order, The, 73
Far Eastern
  grouping, 79
  problems, 72
  regional security system, 76
Fascist-Nazi
  risings in Latin America, 142
  theory of government, 5
Federalism, federalization, federation
  British interest in, 48
  central authority, 140, 144
  citizenship, 172
  Danubian, 36
  French views of, 50
  idea of, 32, 42, 95, 144, 157, 159, 186, 187
Federalist, 32
Federation for Western Europe, A, 141, 157, 180
Finland, 15
Formula of Federation, The, 53
Four Power Treaty, 26, 77
France
  aims, 50
  and Great Britain, 6, 23, 48
  and League, 12, 13, 18, 19, 21, 22, 120, 170
Franco, 23
Funk plan, 83, 84, 88

General Act for the Pacific Settlement of Disputes, 153
Geneva
  post-war, 174
  Protocol, 18, 19
  secretariat, 15

Germany
  economic, 20, 83, 84, 123
  League, 12, 15, 20, 120
  liberal, 136
  post-war, 36, 38, 51, 52
  totalitarianism, 86, 110
Germany—The Voice from Within, 52
Gold standard, 118, 119, 120, 122
Gondra Treaty, 63, 64
Good-neighbor policy, 88
Great Britain
  after 1918, 119
  and France, 6
  and League, 12, 19, 21, 170
  and U.S.A., 7, 10, 11, 13, 91-97, 143-144, 185
  before 1914, 118, 125
  laisser faire, 124, 125
  Parliamentary Labor Party, 48
Greece, 4, 5, 15, 17

Hague, The
  codification at, 1930, 162
  Convention of 1907, 64, 99
  economic and social conference 1940, 132
  Permanent Court of Arbitration, 98
  Permanent Court of International Justice, 15, 16, 39, 51, 77, 78, 98, 100, 102-104, 148-153, 161
Haile Selassie, 21
Hamilton, Alexander, *Federalist,* 32
Havana
  Conference of 1928, 55, 65
  Convention of 1928, 55, 56, 59
  Convention on Commercial Aviation, 60
  Meeting of Foreign Ministers, 61
Henry IV, Grand Design of, 28
Herriot, 19, 29
Hitch and Meade, *Economic Analysis and Policy,* 128
Hitler, Hitlerism, 5, 22, 123, 159, 174
Hoare, Sir Samuel, 21
Holland, 12
Holland, W. L., 73, 73 *footnote,* 74, 76, 79, 80, 116

Holy Roman Empire, 109
Hull, Cordell, 10
Hungary, 16
Huxley, Julian, 34, 189

India, 74, 79, 80
Indo-China, 74
Indonesian Union, 75, 76, 79
Institute of Pacific Relations
  Banff Conference, 76
  Virginia Beach Meeting, 72
Inter-American (see Pan American)
  Bank, 61, 62, 131
  Conference of 1936, 59, 68
  Consultative Committee, Permanent Court of, 67
  Court, 65
  Development Commission, 61, 131
  Financial, Economic and Advisory Committee, 61, 62, 131
  Labor Institute, 63
  Neutrality Committee, 67
  system, 55, 57, 69, 189
  trade, 61
International
  Commission for Air Navigation, 160, 192
  Conciliation, 123, 127 *footnotes*
  Conference of American Jurists, 66, 69
  Conferences of American States, 57, 58, 59
  Economic Reconstruction, report on, 122
  Joint Commission, 106
  judicial establishment, 101, 148, 150, 153, 154
  Justice, Permanent Court of, 15, 16, 39, 51, 77, 78, 98, 100, 104, 115, 148-153, 161
  Labor Organization, 16, 35, 63, 102, 111, 115, 132, 165, 169, 192
  law
    amendments to, 104
    codification, 65, 66, 162
    weaknesses of, 98, 99, 100, 103, 105, 106, 166
  legislative, 13

International—(*Continued*)
  navy, 38
  police, 13
  secretariat, 171, 172
  Staff College, 135, 176
  trade, 72, 119, 121
  unions, 28
Isolated America, 33, 52, 53, 77, 139
Isolationism, 48, 89, 93, 94
Italy, 5
  and Ethiopia, 21
  and Greece, 17
  and League, 12, 13, 17
  post-war, 37
  totalitarian, 86

Janina, 17
Japan
  and Axis New Order, 5, 85, 86
  and League, 13, 20, 26
  and Washington Treaty, 26
  post-war plans for, 73, 74, 77
Jennings, W. Ivor, *A Federation for Western Europe*, 49, 153, 157, 180
Joint Defense Board, 89, 142

Lamas, Dr. Saavedra, 67
Latin America, progress of Axis Powers, 62
Laval, 21, 22
Law, (*see also International law*)
  binding on nations, 166
  of nationality, 162
  of responsibility, 162
  of territorial waters, 162
Layton plan, 190
League of Nations
  Assembly, 15, 18, 169
  Briand's European Federal Union, 29-31
  codification, 162
  Covenant, 14, 15, 24, 160, 170
  failures of, 8, 17-24, 36, 108, 114, 120, 162, 163, 186
  organized force, 105
Peace Conference, 4
Scelle plan, 52
Secretariat, 170, 171

INDEX

League of Nations—(*Continued*)
successes of, 15-17, 115, 131, 186
Treaty of Versailles, 3
League of the Western Hemisphere, 69
Lease-Lend Act, 89
L'Esprit International, 52
Le Problème du Fédéralisme, 50, 155, 187 footnote
Les Nouveaux Cahiers, 50
Lima Conference of 1938, 63
Lithuania, loss of Vilna, 17
Locarno Agreements, 19, 22, 120
London, controller of credit, 118

Majority decision, 159-162
Manchukuo, 163
Manchuria, 20, 163, 164
Mandates Commission, 39
Maritain, Jacques, "Europe and the Federal Idea," 50
Meade, J. E.
Economic Analysis and Policy, 125, 128
Economic Bases of a Durable Peace, 125
Memel, 23
Memorandum on a Federation of Free Peoples, 53
Mexico City Convention of 1901, 60
Mills, Lennox, *Nationalism and Government in Southeast Asia*, 74 footnote
Mixed Arbitral Tribunals, 106
Mohammedan League, 190
Monroe Doctrine, 68, 141
Montevideo Conference, 63, 66, 141
Morley, Felix, "The Formula of Federation," 53
Munich, 23
Mussolini, 17, 21

National
interest, safeguard for, 165
planning, 126
sovereignty, 14
trade restrictions, 126

Nationalism and Government in Southeast Asia, 74 footnote
Nationalism
in Southeast Asia, 74
obstacle to progress, 111, 114
Naval
bases, 89
zones, 38, 143
Nazi
master-race doctrine, 5, 6, 7, 86
plans for Europe, 84, 88, 110, 130, 190
regime in Germany, 123
Near Eastern federation, 36
Netherlands Indies, 74
Neutrality
Acts of 1935-1939, 89
Pan American policy of, 141
transition from, 93
New Commonwealth Institute of London, 137, 148
New World Order, The, 40, 45, 124 footnote, 193
New Zealand, 80
Nine Power Treaty (or Pact), 26, 33, 72, 77, 78, 142, 143
Nonintervention, Spanish civil war, 22
Nonrecognition, Stimson doctrine of, 27
North Atlantic Fisheries Case, 148
Northern federation, 36

Ogdensburg Agreement, 89, 142
Ottawa Agreements, 10, 122

Pacific
Conference, 33
Court, 81, 82
organization of, 33, 77, 78, 80
Pact of, 76
Powers, 41
prerequisites to peace in, 77, 78
zone, 38
Pact of Paris, 27, 65
Panama
Conference of 1826, 58
Meeting of Foreign Ministers at, 1939, 61, 67, 68

Pan American
  articles of association, 54-56
  Bulletin, 60
  Conciliation Conventions, 153
  Conferences, 54-70
  joint force, 141, 142
  neutrality policy, 141
  Sanitary Bureau, 62
  Union, 54, 56, 57, 58, 60, 65, 68, 170
Pan Americanism, products of, 60
Pan European Union, 29
Papacy, 109
Paris
  and League, 13
  Convention of 1919, 60
  Pact of, 27, 65
Peace
  Conference of 1919, 4, 12
  economic approach to, 116
  in Pacific, 72, 142
  propaganda for, 136
Peace Aims, 9, 10, 85, 90, 190
Peace by Federation, 49
Peace in Our Time? 53
Peffer, Nathaniel, *Prerequisites to Peace in the Far East,* 73
Permanent Cartel Commission, 39
Permanent Court of Arbitration, 98
Permanent Court of International Justice, 15, 16, 39, 51, 77, 78, 98, 100, 102, 103, 104, 115, 148-153, 161
Permanent Inter-American Consultative Committee, 67
Permanent Joint Defense Board, 89, 142
Philippines, 74
Poincaré, defeat of, 19
Poland, 4, 15, 17, 23
Police *(see Supranational)*
Politique Etrangère, 50, 155, 187 footnote
Prerequisites to Peace in the Far East, 73
Problem of the Twentieth Century, The, 137

Problems of the Pacific, 72, 77
Proportional representation, 157, 158, 168

Rappard, William, 52
Rearmament, 123
Reconstruction of World Trade, The, 120 footnote, 126
Regional
  associations, 34, 164, 173
  economic machinery, 131
  federations, 129, 140
  organization, Pan American, 70
  police, 139
  tribunals, 104
Rhine, Rhineland, 18, 22
Roosevelt
  aid to Britain, 90
  joint declaration, 10
    Atlantic Charter, 10, 11, 97, 185
  peace aims of, 9, 85, 86, 90
Ruhr, 19, 120

Saar Territory, 16
St. Pierre, 53
Sanctions, 21, 22
Santiago Conference of 1923, 55, 63
Saurat, Denis, "French Aims," 50
Scandinavia, 12
Scelle, Georges, "Le Problème du Fédéralisme," 50, 51, 153, 155, 187, 188
Schmidt, Hans, "Germany—The from Voice Within," 52
Simon, Sir John, 20
Sino-Japanese conciliation commission, 78
Smoot-Hawley tariff, 122
Smuts, General, 8
Socialism, 40, 193, 194
Some Considerations on the Future Reconstruction of Peace Machinery in the Pacific, 76, 78
South China Sea, 76
Southeast Asia, 74
Sovereignty, 30, 103-105, 108-111, 183

INDEX

Spain, civil war, 22
Stabilization of pound, 121
Staley, Eugene, 116 *footnote*, 125, 126, 127, 132
State
 blocs, 158
 economic control, 124
 Houses, 156
 inefficient instrument, 98, 112, 113
 theory of, 104, 112
Stimson, doctrine of nonrecognition, 27
Streit, Clarence, *Union Now*, 42, 44-47, 92, 187
Stresemann, G., 19
Sudetenland, 23
Sully, Duc de, 28, 53
Supranational
 association, 94
 authority, 6, 36, 112, 117
 body, Japan's proposal of, 13
 community, 105, 113, 137
 courts, 152
 dictatorships (Nazi), 7
 economic co-ordination, 125, 127
 institutions, 131, 194
 law, 104, 107, 159
 organization, 7, 17, 83, 86, 94, 96, 136, 155, 159, 173
 police, 33, 36, 101, 105, 138, 139, 144, 145
Supreme Council, 37
Supreme World Court, 104
Sweden, 15

Takaki, *Some Considerations on the Future Reconstruction of Peace Machinery in the Pacific*, 76, 78
Third Reich, 83
Thompson, Virginia, *Nationalism and Government in Southeast Asia*, 74 *footnote*
Tokyo Imperial University, 76
Totalitarianism, 86
Trusteeship, principle of, 39, 78, 180, 181
Turkey, 15

Union Now, 31, 42, 44, 47, 92
U.S.S.R.
 post-war influence, 86
 regional group, 34, 37, 52, 189
 Second World War, 4, 5
United States
 aid to democracies, 89, 90, 93
 and Great Britain, 7, 10, 11, 13, 91-97, 143-144, 185
 and League of Nations, 6, 13, 18, 24, 143
 economic dictatorship, 125
 inter-American role, 60, 67-70
 isolationism, 93
 Senate, 156
 tariff rise, 1922, 120
United States of Europe, 31, 151
United States of Europe, The, 52, 179
Universal
 association, 32, 96, 97, 159
 community, 33, 44
 federation, 95, 144, 159, 187
 police force, 144
 suffrage, 158
 supranational law, 104, 107, 159
Universal Postal Union, 160
Universal Telegraph and Postal Union, 114
Upper Silesia, 17

Versailles, Treaty of, 3, 18, 22, 102
Vilna, 17

War
 condemnation of, 65
 English declaration of, 23
 French declaration of, 23
 renounced as national policy, 27
 self-defense, 100
Warburg, James P., *Peace in Our Time?* 53
Washington
 Conference of 1889, 58
 of 1929, 59
 Convention of 1929, 63
 on Arbitration, 63
 on Conciliation, 63

Washington—(*Continued*)
  disarmament conference, 25
  Treaty, 25, 26, 65
Welles, Sumner, 10
Wells, H. G., *New World Order*, 40, 45, 193
Western
  Atlantic, 38
  federation, 140, 141
  Powers, 73, 79
Why Britain Is at War, 49
Wilson, President Woodrow, 12
World association (or community), 41, 97, 114
World Commonwealth
  difference from League, 169
  establishment of, 80, 130
  framework of, 189
    Assembly, 132, 169, 191
    Central Bank, 133, 175
    Development Commission, 134
    Economic and Financial Organization, 132, 134, 191
    Governing Body, 133
    Intellectual Co-operation, Commission on, 192

World Commonwealth—(*Continued*)
  framework of—(*Continued*)
    Mandates Commission, 182
    Migration and Settlement Commission, 134
    Secretariat, 173, 175
    Social Organization, 134, 192
    Territorial Administration, Commission for, 183, 192
    Trade Commission, 133
    Transit and Communications, Commission on, 192
    World Court, 191
      objections to, 190
  universal association, 166
    assembly of, 159, 166, 167
World Economy in Transition, 125, 126
World Trade Commission, 175
World War I, 3, 117, 119
World War II, 23, 123

Yokota, 76, 78

Zeitgeist, 52

THE I. P. R. INQUIRY SERIES

At the invitation of the Institute of Pacific Relations, scholars in many countries have been engaged since early in 1938 in the preparation of studies forming part of an Inquiry into the problems arising from the conflict in the Far East. The purpose of this Inquiry is to provide an impartial and constructive analysis of the major issues which may have to be considered in any future adjustment of international relations in that area.

The studies include an account of the economic and political conditions which led to the outbreak of fighting in July 1937, with respect to China, to Japan and to the other foreign Powers concerned; an evaluation of developments during the war period which affect the policies of all the Powers in relation to the Far Eastern situation; and, finally, an estimate of the principal political, economic and social conditions which may be expected in a post-war period, the possible forms of adjustment which might be applied under these conditions, and the effects of such adjustments upon the countries concerned.

The Inquiry does not propose to "document" a specific plan for dealing with the Far Eastern situation. Its aim is to present information in forms which will be useful to those who lack the time or expert knowledge to study the vast amount of material now appearing in a number of languages. A list of Inquiry studies already completed appears on the following page.

SOME OTHER STUDIES ALREADY COMPLETED IN THE I. P. R. INQUIRY SERIES

JAPANESE INDUSTRY: ITS RECENT DEVELOPMENT AND PRESENT CONDITION, by G. C. Allen, Brunner Professor of Economic Science, University of Liverpool. 124 pages. $1.00

ECONOMIC SHANGHAI: HOSTAGE TO POLITICS: 1937-1941, by Robert W. Barnett, International Secretariat, Institute of Pacific Relations.
210 pages. $2.00

AMERICAN POLICY IN THE FAR EAST, 1931-1941, Revised Edition, by T. A. Bisson, Foreign Policy Association. With a supplementary chapter by Miriam S. Farley, American Council, Institute of Pacific Relations.
208 pages. $1.75

GERMAN INTERESTS AND POLICIES IN THE FAR EAST, by Kurt Bloch, American Council, Institute of Pacific Relations. 75 pages. $1.00

JAPAN SINCE 1931, by Hugh Borton, Assistant Professor of Japanese, Columbia University. 141 pages. $1.25

THE CHINESE ARMY, by Major Evans Fordyce Carlson, United States Marine Corps, Recently Resigned. 139 pages. $1.00

FAR EASTERN TRADE OF THE UNITED STATES, by Ethel B. Dietrich, Professor of Economics, Mt. Holyoke College. 116 pages. $1.00

GOVERNMENT IN JAPAN, by Charles B. Fahs, Assistant Professor of Oriental Affairs, Pomona and Claremont Colleges. 114 pages. $1.00

THE PROBLEM OF JAPANESE TRADE EXPANSION IN THE POST-WAR SITUATION, by Miriam S. Farley, American Council, Institute of Pacific Relations.
93 pages. $1.00

BRITISH RELATIONS WITH CHINA: 1931-1939, by Irving S. Friedman, International Secretariat, Institute of Pacific Relations. 256 pages. $2.00

FRENCH INTERESTS AND POLICIES IN THE FAR EAST, by Roger Lévy, Chargé de Cours École Nationale de la France d'Outremer; Guy Lacam, Formerly Director of the Economic Department of the Bank of Indo-China; Andrew Roth, International Secretariat, Institute of Pacific Relations.
209 pages. $2.00

CANADA AND THE FAR EAST, 1940, by A. R. M. Lower, Professor of History, United College, University of Manitoba. 152 pages. $1.25

NEW ZEALAND'S INTERESTS AND POLICIES IN THE FAR EAST, by Ian F. G. Milner, New Zealand Institute for Educational Research.
131 pages. $1.00

JAPAN'S EMERGENCE AS A MODERN STATE, by E. Herbert Norman, International Secretariat, Institute of Pacific Relations. 254 pages. $2.00

PREREQUISITES TO PEACE IN THE FAR EAST, by Nathaniel Peffer, Associate Professor of International Relations, Columbia University.
121 pages. $1.00

AUSTRALIA'S INTERESTS AND POLICIES IN THE FAR EAST, by Jack Shepherd, International Secretariat, Institute of Pacific Relations. 212 pages, $2.00

ITALY'S INTERESTS AND POLICIES IN THE FAR EAST, by Frank M. Tamagna, Instructor in Economics, Xavier University. 91 pages. $1.00

STRUGGLE FOR NORTH CHINA, by George E. Taylor, Assistant Professor of Oriental Studies, University of Washington. 247 pages. $2.00

LEGAL PROBLEMS IN THE FAR EASTERN CONFLICT, by Quincy Wright, Professor of Law, University of Chicago; H. Lauterpacht, Professor of International Law, Cambridge University; Edwin M. Borchard, Professor of International Law, Yale University, and Phoebe Morrison, Research Associate in International Law, Yale University.
211 pages. $2.00